THE PELICAN SHAKESPEARE
GENERAL EDITORS

STEPHEN ORGEL
A. R. BRAUNMULLER

The Life of King Henry the Eighth

Ellen Terry as a bravura Queen Katherine at the Lyceum
Theatre, London, 1892. Cardinal Wolsey was played by
Henry Irving, the king by William Terriss; in the small role
of Thomas Cromwell appeared the nineteen-year-old Edward
Gordon Craig, Ellen Terry's son, who subsequently became
one of the great modern stage designers. From a sketch
by J. Bernard Partridge in the souvenir program.

William Shakespeare

The Life of King Henry the Eighth

EDITED BY JONATHAN CREWE

PENGUIN BOOKS

PENGUIN BOOKS
Published by the Penguin Group
Penguin Putnam Inc., 375 Hudson Street,
New York, New York 10014, U.S.A.
Penguin Books Ltd, 27 Wrights Lane, London W8 5TZ, England
Penguin Books Australia Ltd, Ringwood, Victoria, Australia
Penguin Books Canada Ltd, 10 Alcorn Avenue,
Toronto, Ontario, Canada M4V 3B2
Penguin Books (N.Z.) Ltd, 182–190 Wairau Road,
Auckland 10, New Zealand

Penguin Books Ltd, Registered Offices:
Harmondsworth, Middlesex, England

The Life of King Henry the Eighth edited by F. David Hoeniger
published in the United States of America in Penguin Books 1966
Revised edition published 1981
This new edition edited by Jonathan Crewe published 2001

10 9 8 7 6 5 4 3 2 1

LIBRARY OF CONGRESS CATALOGING IN PUBLICATION DATA
Shakespeare, William, 1564–1616.
[King Henry VIII]
Henry VIII / William Shakespeare; edited by Jonathan Crewe.
p. cm. – (The Pelican Shakespeare)
ISBN 0-14-310457-8
1. Henry VIII, King of England, 1491–1547 – Drama. 2. Great
Britain – History – Henry VIII, 1509–1547 – Drama. I. Crewe,
Jonathan V. II. Title. III. Series.
PR2817.A2 C74 2001
822.3'3 – dc21   2001031338

Printed in the United States of America
Set in Adobe Garamond
Designed by Virginia Norey

Contents

Publisher's Note

IT IS ALMOST half a century since the first volumes of the Pelican Shakespeare appeared under the general editorship of Alfred Harbage. The fact that a new edition, rather than simply a revision, has been undertaken reflects the profound changes textual and critical studies of Shakespeare have undergone in the past twenty years. For the new Pelican series, the texts of the plays and poems have been thoroughly revised in accordance with recent scholarship, and in some cases have been entirely reedited. New introductions and notes have been provided in all the volumes. But the new Shakespeare is also designed as a successor to the original series; the previous editions have been taken into account, and the advice of the previous editors has been solicited where it was feasible to do so.

Certain textual features of the new Pelican Shakespeare should be particularly noted. All lines are numbered that contain a word, phrase, or allusion explained in the glossarial notes. In addition, for convenience, every tenth line is also numbered, in italics when no annotation is indicated. The intrusive and often inaccurate place headings inserted by early editors are omitted (as is becoming standard practice), but for the convenience of those who miss them, an indication of locale now appears as the first item in the annotation of each scene.

In the interest of both elegance and utility, each speech prefix is set in a separate line when the speaker's lines are in verse, except when those words form the second half of a verse line. Thus the verse form of the speech is kept visually intact. What is printed as verse and what is printed as prose has, in general, the authority of the original texts. Departures from the original texts in this regard have only the authority of editorial tradition and the judgment of the Pelican editors; and, in a few instances, are admittedly arbitrary.

The Theatrical World

Economic realities determined the theatrical world in which Shakespeare's plays were written, performed, and received. For centuries in England, the primary theatrical tradition was nonprofessional. Craft guilds (or "mysteries") provided religious drama – mystery plays – as part of the celebration of religious and civic festivals, and schools and universities staged classical and neoclassical drama in both Latin and English as part of their curricula. In these forms, drama was established and socially acceptable. Professional theater, in contrast, existed on the margins of society. The acting companies were itinerant; playhouses could be any available space – the great halls of the aristocracy, town squares, civic halls, inn yards, fair booths, or open fields – and income was sporadic, dependent on the passing of the hat or on the bounty of local patrons. The actors, moreover, were considered little better than vagabonds, constantly in danger of arrest or expulsion.

In the late 1560s and 1570s, however, English professional theater began to gain respectability. Wealthy aristocrats fond of drama – the Lord Admiral, for example, or the Lord Chamberlain – took acting companies under their protection so that the players technically became members of their households and were no longer subject to arrest as homeless or masterless men. Permanent theaters were first built at this time as well, allowing the companies to control and charge for entry to their performances.

Shakespeare's livelihood, and the stunning artistic explosion in which he participated, depended on pragmatic and architectural effort. Professional theater requires ways to restrict access to its offerings; if it does not, and admission fees cannot be charged, the actors do not get paid, the costumes go to a pawnbroker, and there is no such thing as a professional, ongoing theatrical tradition. The answer to that economic need arrived in the late 1560s and 1570s with the creation of the so-called public or amphitheater playhouse. Recent discoveries indicate that the precursor of the Globe playhouse in London (where Shakespeare's mature plays were presented) and the Rose theater (which presented Christopher Marlowe's plays and some of Shakespeare's earliest ones) was the Red Lion theater of 1567. Archaeological studies of the foundations of the Rose and Globe theaters have revealed that the open-air theater of the 1590s and later was probably a polygonal building with fourteen to twenty or twenty-four sides, multistoried, from 75 to 100 feet in diameter, with a raised, partly covered "thrust" stage that projected into a group of standing patrons, or "groundlings," and a covered gallery, seating up to 2,500 or more (very crowded) spectators.

These theaters might have been about half full on any given day, though the audiences were larger on holidays or when a play was advertised, as old and new were, through printed playbills posted around London. The metropolitan area's late-Tudor, early-Stuart population (circa 1590-1620) has been estimated at about 150,000 to 250,000. It has been supposed that in the mid-1590s there were about 15,000 spectators per week at the public theaters; thus, as many as 10 percent of the local population went to the theater regularly. Consequently, the theaters' repertories – the plays available for this experienced and frequent audience – had to change often: in the month between September 15 and October 15, 1595, for instance, the Lord Admiral's Men performed twenty-eight times in eighteen different plays.

Since natural light illuminated the amphitheaters' stages, performances began between noon and two o'clock and ran without a break for two or three hours. They often concluded with a jig, a fencing display, or some other nondramatic exhibition. Weather conditions determined the season for the amphitheaters: plays were performed every day (including Sundays, sometimes, to clerical dismay) except during Lent – the forty days before Easter – or periods of plague, or sometimes during the summer months when law courts were not in session and the most affluent members of the audience were not in London.

To a modern theatergoer, an amphitheater stage like that of the Rose or Globe would appear an unfamiliar mixture of plainness and elaborate decoration. Much of the structure was carved or painted, sometimes to imitate marble; elsewhere, as under the canopy projecting over the stage, to represent the stars and the zodiac. Appropriate painted canvas pictures (of Jerusalem, for example, if the play was set in that city) were apparently hung on the wall behind the acting area, and tragedies were accompanied by black hangings, presumably something like crepe festoons or bunting. Although these theaters did not employ what we would call scenery, early modern spectators saw numerous large props, such as the "bar" at which a prisoner stood during a trial, the "mossy bank" where lovers reclined, an arbor for amorous conversation, a chariot, gallows, tables, trees, beds, thrones, writing desks, and so forth. Audiences might learn a scene's location from a sign (reading "Athens," for example) carried across the stage (as in Bertolt Brecht's twentieth-century productions). Equally captivating (and equally irritating to the theater's enemies) were the rich costumes and personal props the actors used: the most valuable items in the surviving theatrical inventories are the swords, gowns, robes, crowns, and other items worn or carried by the performers.

Magic appealed to Shakespeare's audiences as much as it does to us today, and the theater exploited many deceptive and spectacular devices. A winch in the loft above the stage, called "the heavens," could lower and raise actors playing gods, goddesses, and other supernatural figures to and from the main acting area, just as one or more trapdoors permitted entrances and exits to and from the area, called "hell," beneath the stage. Actors wore elementary makeup such as wigs, false beards, and face paint, and they employed pig's bladders filled with animal blood to make wounds seem more real. They had rudimentary but effective ways of pretending to behead or hang a person. Supernumeraries (stagehands or actors not needed in a particular scene) could make thunder sounds (by shaking a metal sheet or rolling an iron ball down a chute) and show lightning (by blowing inflammable resin through tubes into a flame). Elaborate fireworks enhanced the effects of dragons flying through the air or imitated such celestial phenomena as comets, shooting stars, and multiple suns. Horses' hoofbeats, bells (located perhaps in the tower above the stage), trumpets and drums, clocks, cannon shots and gunshots, and the like were common sound effects. And the music of viols, cornets, oboes, and recorders was a regular feature of theatrical performances.

For two relatively brief spans, from the late 1570s to 1590 and from 1599 to 1614, the amphitheaters competed with the so-called private, or indoor, theaters, which originated as, or later represented themselves as, educational institutions training boys as singers for church services and court performances. These indoor theaters had two features that were distinct from the amphitheaters': their personnel and their playing spaces. The amphitheaters' adult companies included both adult men, who played the male roles, and boys, who played the female roles; the private, or indoor, theater companies, on the other hand, were entirely composed of boys aged about 8 to 16, who were, or could pretend to be, candidates for singers in a church or a royal boys' choir. (Until 1660, professional theatrical companies included no women.) The playing space would appear much more familiar to modern audiences than the long-vanished amphitheaters; the later indoor theaters were, in fact, the ancestors of the typical modern theater. They were enclosed spaces, usually rectangular, with the stage filling one end of the rectangle and the audience arrayed in seats or benches across (and sometimes lining) the building's longer axis. These spaces staged plays less frequently than the public theaters (perhaps only once a week) and held far fewer spectators than the amphitheaters: about 200 to 600, as opposed to 2,500 or more. Fewer patrons mean a smaller gross income, unless each pays more. Not surprisingly, then, private theaters charged higher prices than the amphitheaters, probably sixpence, as opposed to a penny for the cheapest entry.

Protected from the weather, the indoor theaters presented plays later in the day than the amphitheaters, and used artificial illumination – candles in sconces or candelabra. But candles melt, and need replacing, snuffing, and trimming, and these practical requirements may have been part of the reason the indoor theaters introduced breaks in the performance, the intermission so dear to the heart of theatergoers and to the pocketbooks of theater concessionaires ever since. Whether motivated by the need to tend to the candles or by the entrepreneurs' wishing to sell oranges and liquor, or both, the indoor theaters eventually established the modern convention of the noncontinuous performance. In the early modern "private" theater, musical performances apparently filled the intermissions, which in Stuart theater jargon seem to have been called "acts."

At the end of the first decade of the seventeenth century, the distinction between public amphitheaters and private indoor companies ceased. For various cultural, political, and economic reasons, individual companies gained control of both the public, open-air theaters and the indoor ones, and companies mixing adult men and boys took over the formerly "private" theaters. Despite the death of the boys' companies and of their highly innovative theaters (for which such luminous playwrights as Ben Jonson, George Chapman, and John Marston wrote), their playing spaces and conventions had an immense impact on subsequent plays: not merely for the intervals (which stressed the artistic and architectonic importance of "acts"), but also because they introduced political and social satire as a popular dramatic ingredient, even in tragedy, and a wider range of actorly effects, encouraged by their more intimate playing spaces.

Even the briefest sketch of the Shakespearean theatrical world would be incomplete without some comment on the social and cultural dimensions of theaters and playing in the period. In an intensely hierarchical and status-conscious society, professional actors and their ventures had hardly any respectability; as we have indicated, to protect themselves against laws designed to curb vagabondage and the increase of masterless men, actors resorted to the near-fiction that they were the servants of noble masters, and wore their distinctive livery. Hence the company for which Shakespeare wrote in the 1590s called itself the Lord Chamberlain's Men and pretended that the public, money-getting performances were in fact rehearsals for private performances before that high court official. From 1598, the Privy Council had licensed theatrical companies, and after 1603, with the accession of King James I, the companies gained explicit royal protection, just as the Queen's Men had for a time under Queen Elizabeth. The Chamberlain's Men became the King's Men, and the other companies were patronized by the other members of the royal family.

These designations were legal fictions that half-concealed an important economic and social development, the evolution away from the theater's organization on the model of the guild, a self-regulating confraternity of individual artisans, into a proto-capitalist organization. Shakespeare's company became a joint-stock company, where persons who supplied capital and, in some cases,

such as Shakespeare's, capital and talent, employed themselves and others in earning a return on that capital. This
development meant that actors and theater companies
were outside both the traditional guild structures, which
required some form of civic or royal charter, and the feu-
dal household organization of master-and-servant. This
anomalous, maverick social and economic condition
made theater companies practically unruly and potentially even dangerous; consequently, numerous official
bodies – including the London metropolitan and ecclesi-
astical authorities as well as, occasionally, the royal court
itself – tried, without much success, to control and even
to disband them.

Public officials had good reason to want to close the
theaters: they were attractive nuisances – they drew often
riotous crowds, they were always noisy, and they could be
politically offensive and socially insubordinate. Until the
Civil War, however, anti-theatrical forces failed to shut
down professional theater, for many reasons – limited
surveillance and few police powers, tensions or outright
hostilities among the agencies that sought to check or
channel theatrical activity, and lack of clear policies for
control. Another reason must have been the theaters' un-
deniable popularity. Curtailing any activity enjoyed by
such a substantial percentage of the population was diffi-
cult, as various Roman emperors attempting to limit cir-
cuses had learned, and the Tudor-Stuart audience was not
merely large, it was socially diverse and included women.
The prevalence of public entertainment in this period
has been underestimated. In fact, fairs, holidays, games,
sporting events, the equivalent of modern parades, freak
shows, and street exhibitions all abounded, but the theater was the most widely and frequently available entertainment to which people of every class had access. That
fact helps account both for its quantity and for the fear
and anger it aroused.

WILLIAM SHAKESPEARE OF
STRATFORD-UPON-AVON, GENTLEMAN

Many people have said that we know very little about William Shakespeare's life – pinheads and postcards are often mentioned as appropriately tiny surfaces on which to record the available information. More imaginatively and perhaps more correctly, Ralph Waldo Emerson wrote, "Shakespeare is the only biographer of Shakespeare. . . . So far from Shakespeare's being the least known, he is the one person in all modern history fully known to us."

In fact, we know more about Shakespeare's life than we do about almost any other English writer's of his era. His last will and testament (dated March 25, 1616) survives, as do numerous legal contracts and court documents involving Shakespeare as principal or witness, and parish records in Stratford and London. Shakespeare appears quite often in official records of King James's royal court, and of course Shakespeare's name appears on numerous title pages and in the written and recorded words of his literary contemporaries Robert Greene, Henry Chettle, Francis Meres, John Davies of Hereford, Ben Jonson, and many others. Indeed, if we make due allowance for the bloating of modern, run-of-the-mill bureaucratic records, more information has survived over the past four hundred years about William Shakespeare of Stratford-upon-Avon, Warwickshire, than is likely to survive in the next four hundred years about any reader of these words.

What we do not have are entire categories of information – Shakespeare's private letters or diaries, drafts and revisions of poems and plays, critical prefaces or essays, commendatory verse for other writers' works, or instructions guiding his fellow actors in their performances, for instance – that we imagine would help us understand and appreciate his surviving writings. For all we know, many such data never existed as written records. Many literary and theatrical critics, not knowing what might once have existed, more or less cheerfully accept the situation; some even make a theoretical virtue of it by claiming that such data are irrelevant to understanding and interpreting the plays and poems.

So, what do we know about William Shakespeare, the man responsible for thirty-seven or perhaps more plays, more than 150 sonnets, two lengthy narrative poems, and some shorter poems?

While many families by the name of Shakespeare (or some variant spelling) can be identified in the English Midlands as far back as the twelfth century, it seems likely that the dramatist's grandfather, Richard, moved to Snitterfield, a town not far from Stratford-upon-Avon, sometime before 1529. In Snitterfield, Richard Shakespeare leased farmland from the very wealthy Robert Arden. By 1552, Richard's son John had moved to a large house on Henley Street in Stratford-upon-Avon, the house that stands today as "The Birthplace." In Stratford, John Shakespeare traded as a glover, dealt in wool, and lent money at interest; he also served in a variety of civic posts, including "High Bailiff," the municipality's equivalent of mayor. In 1557, he married Robert Arden's youngest daughter, Mary. Mary and John had four sons – William was the oldest – and four daughters, of whom only Joan outlived her most celebrated sibling. William was baptized (an event entered in the Stratford parish church records) on April 26, 1564, and it has become customary, without any good factual support, to suppose he was born on April 23, which happens to be the feast day of Saint George, patron saint of England, and is also the date on which he died, in 1616. Shakespeare married Anne Hathaway in 1582, when he was eighteen and she was twenty-six; their first child was born five months later. It has been generally assumed that the marriage was enforced and subsequently unhappy, but these are only assumptions; it has been estimated, for instance, that up to one third of Elizabethan brides were pregnant when they married. Anne and William Shakespeare had three children: Susanna, who married a prominent local physician, John Hall; and the twins Hamnet, who died young in 1596, and Judith, who married Thomas Quiney – apparently a rather shady individual. The name Hamnet was unusual but not unique: he and his twin sister were named for their godparents, Shakespeare's neighbors Hamnet and Judith Sadler. Shakespeare's father died in 1601 (the year of *Hamlet*), and Mary Arden Shakespeare died in 1608 (the year of *Coriolanus*). William Shakespeare's last surviving direct descendant was his granddaughter Elizabeth Hall, who died in 1670.

Between the birth of the twins in 1585 and a clear reference to Shakespeare as a practicing London dramatist in Robert Greene's sensationalizing, satiric pamphlet, *Greene's Groatsworth of Wit* (1592), there is no record of where William Shakespeare was or what he was doing. These seven so-called lost years have been imaginatively filled by scholars and other students of Shakespeare: some think he traveled to Italy, or fought in the Low Countries, or studied law or medicine, or worked as an apprentice actor/writer, and so on to even more fanciful possibilities. Whatever the biographical facts for those "lost" years, Greene's nasty remarks in 1592 testify to professional envy and to the fact that Shakespeare already had a successful career in London. Speaking to his fellow playwrights, Greene warns both generally and specifically:

> . . . trust them [actors] not: for there is an upstart crow, beautified with our feathers, that with his tiger's heart wrapped in a player's hide supposes he is as well able to bombast out a blank verse as the best of you; and being an absolute Johannes Factotum, is in his own conceit the only Shake-scene in a country.

The passage mimics a line from *3 Henry VI* (hence the play must have been performed before Greene wrote) and seems to say that "Shake-scene" is both actor and playwright, a jack-of-all-trades. That same year, Henry Chettle protested Greene's remarks in *Kind-Heart's Dream*, and each of the next two years saw the publication of poems – *Venus and Adonis* and *The Rape of Lucrece*, respectively – publicly ascribed to (and dedicated by) Shakespeare. Early in 1595 he was named one of the senior members of a prominent acting company, the Lord Chamberlain's Men, when they received payment for court performances during the 1594 Christmas season.

Clearly, Shakespeare had achieved both success and reputation in London. In 1596, upon Shakespeare's application, the College of Arms granted his father the now-familiar coat of arms he had taken the first steps to obtain almost twenty years before, and in 1598, John's son – now permitted to call himself "gentleman" – took a 10 percent share in the new Globe playhouse. In 1597, he bought a substantial bourgeois house, called New Place, in Stratford – the garden remains, but Shakespeare's house, several times rebuilt, was torn down in 1759 – and over the next few years Shakespeare spent large sums buying land and making other investments in the town and its environs. Though he worked in London, his family remained in Stratford, and he seems always to have considered Stratford the home he would eventually return to. Something approaching a disinterested appreciation of Shakespeare's popular and professional status appears in Francis Meres's *Palladis Tamia* (1598), a not especially imaginative and perhaps therefore persuasive record of literary reputations. Reviewing contemporary English writers, Meres lists the titles of many of Shakespeare's plays, including one not now known, *Love's Labor's Won,* and praises his "mellifluous & hony-tongued" "sugred Sonnets," which were then circulating in manuscript (they were first collected in 1609). Meres describes Shakespeare as "one of the best" English playwrights of both comedy and tragedy. In *Remains . . . Concerning Britain* (1605),

William Camden – a more authoritative source than the imitative Meres – calls Shakespeare one of the "most pregnant witts of these our times" and joins him with such writers as Chapman, Daniel, Jonson, Marston, and Spenser. During the first decades of the seventeenth century, publishers began to attribute numerous play quartos, including some non-Shakespearean ones, to Shakespeare, either by name or initials, and we may assume that they deemed Shakespeare's name and supposed authorship, true or false, commercially attractive.

For the next ten years or so, various records show Shakespeare's dual career as playwright and man of the theater in London, and as an important local figure in Stratford. In 1608-9 his acting company – designated the "King's Men" soon after King James had succeeded Queen Elizabeth in 1603 – rented, refurbished, and opened a small interior playing space, the Blackfriars theater, in London, and Shakespeare was once again listed as a substantial sharer in the group of proprietors of the playhouse. By May 11, 1612, however, he describes himself as a Stratford resident in a London lawsuit – an indication that he had withdrawn from day-to-day professional activity and returned to the town where he had always had his main financial interests. When Shakespeare bought a substantial residential building in London, the Blackfriars Gatehouse, close to the theater of the same name, on March 10, 1613, he is recorded as William Shakespeare "of Stratford upon Avon in the county of Warwick, gentleman," and he named several London residents as the building's trustees. Still, he continued to participate in theatrical activity: when the new Earl of Rutland needed an allegorical design to bear as a shield, or *impresa,* at the celebration of King James's Accession Day, March 24, 1613, the earl's accountant recorded a payment of 44 shillings to Shakespeare for the device with its motto.

For the last few years of his life, Shakespeare evidently

concentrated his activities in the town of his birth. Most of the final records concern business transactions in Stratford, ending with the notation of his death on April 23, 1616, and burial in Holy Trinity Church, Stratford-upon-Avon.

THE QUESTION OF AUTHORSHIP

The history of ascribing Shakespeare's plays (the poems do not come up so often) to someone else began, as it continues, peculiarly. The earliest published claim that someone else wrote Shakespeare's plays appeared in an 1856 article by Delia Bacon in the American journal *Putnam's Monthly* – although an Englishman, Thomas Wilmot, had shared his doubts in private (even secretive) conversations with friends near the end of the eighteenth century. Bacon's was a sad personal history that ended in madness and poverty, but the year after her article, she published, with great difficulty and the bemused assistance of Nathaniel Hawthorne (then United States Consul in Liverpool, England), her *Philosophy of the Plays of Shakspere Unfolded.* This huge, ornately written, confusing farrago is almost unreadable; sometimes its intents, to say nothing of its arguments, disappear entirely beneath near-raving, ecstatic writing. Tumbled in with much supposed "philosophy" appear the claims that Francis Bacon (from whom Delia Bacon eventually claimed descent), Walter Ralegh, and several other contemporaries of Shakespeare's had written the plays. The book had little impact except as a ridiculed curiosity.

Once proposed, however, the issue gained momentum among people whose conviction was the greater in proportion to their ignorance of sixteenth- and seventeenth-century English literature, history, and society. Another American amateur, Catherine P. Ashmead Windle, made the next influential contribution to the cause when she published *Report to the British Museum* (1882), wherein she promised to open "the Cipher of Francis Bacon," though what she mostly offers, in the words of S. Schoenbaum, is "demented allegorizing." An entire new cottage industry grew from Windle's suggestion that the texts contain hidden, cryptographically discoverable ciphers – "clues" – to their authorship; and today there are not only books devoted to the putative ciphers, but also pamphlets, journals, and newsletters.

Although Baconians have led the pack of those seeking a substitute Shakespeare, in *"Shakespeare" Identified* (1920), J. Thomas Looney became the first published "Oxfordian" when he proposed Edward de Vere, seventeenth earl of Oxford, as the secret author of Shakespeare's plays. Also for Oxford and his "authorship" there are today dedicated societies, articles, journals, and books. Less popular candidates – Queen Elizabeth and Christopher Marlowe among them – have had adherents, but the movement seems to have divided into two main contending factions, Baconian and Oxfordian. (For further details on all the candidates for "Shakespeare," see S. Schoenbaum, *Shakespeare's Lives,* 2nd ed., 1991.)

The Baconians, the Oxfordians, and supporters of other candidates have one trait in common – they are snobs. Every pro-Bacon or pro-Oxford tract sooner or later claims that the historical William Shakespeare of Stratford-upon-Avon could not have written the plays because he could not have had the training, the university education, the experience, and indeed the imagination or background their author supposedly possessed. Only a learned genius like Bacon or an aristocrat like Oxford could have written such fine plays. (As it happens, lucky male children of the middle class had access to better education than most aristocrats in Elizabethan England – and Oxford was not particularly well educated.) Shakespeare received in the Stratford grammar school a formal education that would daunt many college graduates today; and popular rival playwrights such as the very learned Ben Jonson and George Chapman, both of whom also lacked university training, achieved great artistic success, without being taken as Bacon or Oxford.

Besides snobbery, one other quality characterizes the authorship controversy: lack of evidence. A great deal of testimony from Shakespeare's time shows that Shakespeare wrote Shakespeare's plays and that his contemporaries recognized them as distinctive and distinctly superior. (Some of that contemporary evidence is collected in E. K. Chambers, *William Shakespeare: A Study of Facts and Problems,* 2 vols., 1930.) Since that testimony comes from Shakespeare's enemies and theatrical competitors as well as from his co-workers and from the Elizabethan equivalent of literary journalists, it seems unlikely that, if any of these sources had known he was a fraud, they would have failed to record that fact.

Books About Shakespeare's Theater

Useful scholarly studies of theatrical life in Shakespeare's day include: G. E. Bentley, *The Jacobean and Caroline Stage,* 7 vols. (1941-68), and the same author's *The Professions of Dramatist and Player in Shakespeare's Time, 1590-1642* (1986); E. K. Chambers, *The Elizabethan Stage,* 4 vols. (1923); R. A. Foakes, *Illustrations of the English Stage, 1580-1642* (1985); Andrew Gurr, *The Shakespearean Stage,* 3rd ed. (1992), and the same author's *Play-going in Shakespeare's London,* 2nd ed. (1996); Edwin Nungezer, *A Dictionary of Actors* (1929); Carol Chillington Rutter, ed., *Documents of the Rose Playhouse* (1984).

Books About Shakespeare's Life

The following books provide scholarly, documented accounts of Shakespeare's life: G. E. Bentley, *Shakespeare: A Biographical Handbook* (1961); E. K. Chambers, *William Shakespeare: A Study of Facts and Problems,* 2 vols. (1930); S. Schoenbaum, *William Shakespeare: A Compact*

Documentary Life (1977); and *Shakespeare's Lives,* 2nd ed. (1991), by the same author. Many scholarly editions of Shakespeare's complete works print brief compilations of essential dates and events. References to Shakespeare's works up to 1700 are collected in C. M. Ingleby et al., *The Shakespeare Allusion-Book,* rev. ed., 2 vols. (1932).

The Texts of Shakespeare

As far as we know, only one manuscript conceivably in Shakespeare's own hand may (and even this is much disputed) exist: a few pages of a play called *Sir Thomas More*, which apparently was never performed. What we do have, as later readers, performers, scholars, students, are printed texts. The earliest of these survive in two forms: quartos and folios. Quartos (from the Latin for "four") are small books, printed on sheets of paper that were then folded in fours, to make eight double-sided pages. When these were bound together, the result was a squarish, eminently portable volume that sold for the relatively small sum of sixpence (translating in modern terms to about $5.00). In folios, on the other hand, the sheets are folded only once, in half, producing large, impressive volumes taller than they are wide. This was the format for important works of philosophy, science, theology, and literature (the major precedent for a folio Shakespeare was Ben Jonson's *Works*, 1616). The decision to print the works of a popular playwright in folio is an indication of how far up on the social scale the theatrical profession had come during Shakespeare's lifetime. The Shakespeare folio was an expensive book, selling for between fifteen and eighteen shillings, depending on the binding (in modern terms, from about $150 to $180). Twenty Shakespeare plays of the thirty-seven that survive first appeared in quarto, seventeen of which appeared during Shakespeare's lifetime; the rest of the plays are found only in folio.

The First Folio was published in 1623, seven years after Shakespeare's death, and was authorized by his fellow actors, the co-owners of the King's Men. This publication was certainly a mark of the company's enormous respect for Shakespeare; but it was also a way of turning the old plays, most of which were no longer current in the playhouse, into ready money (the folio includes only Shakespeare's plays, not his sonnets or other nondramatic verse). Whatever the motives behind the publication of the folio, the texts it preserves constitute the basis for almost all later editions of the playwright's works. The texts, however, differ from those of the earlier quartos, sometimes in minor respects but often significantly – most strikingly in the two texts of *King Lear,* but also in important ways in *Hamlet, Othello,* and *Troilus and Cressida.* (The variants are recorded in the textual notes to each play in the new Pelican series.) The differences in these texts represent, in a sense, the essence of theater: the texts of plays were initially not intended for publication. They were scripts, designed for the actors to perform – the principal life of the play at this period was in performance. And it follows that in Shakespeare's theater the playwright typically had no say either in how his play was performed or in the disposition of his text – he was an employee of the company. The authoritative figures in the theatrical enterprise were the shareholders in the company, who were for the most part the major actors. They decided what plays were to be done; they hired the playwright and often gave him an outline of the play they wanted him to write. Often, too, the play was a collaboration: the company would retain a group of writers, and parcel out the scenes among them. The resulting script was then the property of the company, and the actors would revise it as they saw fit during the course of putting it on stage. The resulting text belonged to the company. The playwright had no rights in it once he had been paid. (This system survives largely intact in the movie industry, and most of the playwrights of Shakespeare's time were as anonymous as most screenwriters are today.) The script could also, of course, continue to change as the tastes of audiences and the requirements of the actors changed. Many – perhaps most – plays were revised when they were reintroduced after any substantial absence from the repertory, or when they were performed by a company different from the one that originally commissioned the play.

Shakespeare was an exceptional figure in this world because he was not only a shareholder and actor in his company, but also its leading playwright – he was literally his own boss. He had, moreover, little interest in the publication of his plays, and even those that appeared during his lifetime with the authorization of the company show no signs of any editorial concern on the part of the author. Theater was, for Shakespeare, a fluid and supremely responsive medium – the very opposite of the great classic canonical text that has embodied his works since 1623.

The very fluidity of the original texts, however, has meant that Shakespeare has always had to be edited. Here is an example of how problematic the editorial project inevitably is, a passage from the most famous speech in *Romeo and Juliet*, Juliet's balcony soliloquy beginning "O Romeo, Romeo, wherefore art thou Romeo?" Since the eighteenth century, the standard modern text has read,

> What's Montague? It is nor hand, nor foot,
> Nor arm, nor face, nor any other part
> Belonging to a man. O be some other name!
> What's in a name? That which we call a rose
> By any other name would smell as sweet.
>   (II.2.40–44)

Editors have three early texts of this play to work from, two quarto texts and the folio. Here is how the First Quarto (1597) reads:

> Whats *Mountague?* It is nor hand nor foote,
> Nor arme, nor face, nor any other part.
> Whats in a name? That which we call a Rofe,
> By any other name would fmell as fweet:

Here is the Second Quarto (1599):

> Whats *Mountague?* it is nor hand nor foote,
> Nor arme nor face, ô be fome other name
> Belonging to a man.
> Whats in a name that which we call a rofe,
> By any other word would fmell as fweete,

And here is the First Folio (1623):

> What's *Mountague?* it is nor hand nor foote,
> Nor arme, nor face, O be fome other name
> Belonging to a man.
> What? in a names that which we call a Rofe,
> By any other word would fmell as fweete,

There is in fact no early text that reads as our modern text does – and this is the most famous speech in the play. Instead, we have three quite different texts, all of which are clearly some version of the same speech, but none of which seems to us a final or satisfactory version. The transcendently beautiful passage in modern editions is an editorial invention: editors have succeeded in conflating and revising the three versions into something we recognize as great poetry. Is this what Shakespeare "really" wrote? Who can say? What we can say is that Shakespeare always had performance, not a book, in mind.

Books About the Shakespeare Texts

The standard study of the printing history of the First Folio is W. W. Greg, *The Shakespeare First Folio* (1955). J. K. Walton, *The Quarto Copy for the First Folio of Shakespeare*

(1971), is a useful survey of the relation of the quartos to the folio. The second edition of Charlton Hinman's *Norton Facsimile* of the First Folio (1996), with a new introduction by Peter Blayney, is indispensable. Stanley Wells, Gary Taylor, John Jowett, and William Montgomery, *William Shakespeare: A Textual Companion,* keyed to the Oxford text, gives a comprehensive survey of the editorial situation for all the plays and poems.

THE GENERAL EDITORS

Introduction

ALTHOUGH *The Life of King Henry the Eighth* is a remarkable and highly rewarding play, it is underappreciated at present, having been increasingly overshadowed in the twentieth century by Shakespeare's earlier histories, from *Richard II* through *Henry V*. Before the twentieth century, in fact, the play was a popular one, and was regularly performed with notable success. Sir William Davenant revived it after the Restoration in 1660, and made it one of the great spectacle plays of the age – the diarist Samuel Pepys liked it enough to see it twice. Colley Cibber mounted a sumptuous production in 1727 in honor of the coronation of George II, and added a great deal of pageantry, including a coronation scene. Ironically, it was, of course, Anne Bullen, historically doomed to execution, who was crowned. This set piece succeeded so well that it was added to other plays as a pantomime, and in that one season the coronation from *Henry VIII* was performed seventy-five times. David Garrick kept it in the repertory, as did John Philip Kemble; in the nineteenth century there were major productions by William Macready, Charles Kean, and Sir Henry Irving. The great, virtuoso roles (even today practically foolproof in the theater) were those of Wolsey and Queen Katherine, played in Irving's production, in 1892, by Irving himself and Ellen Terry. Sir Herbert Beerbohm Tree's production, in 1910, was considered a theatrical revelation – as one critic put it, "the most gorgeous thing ever attempted in this country in that line of staging."* With its elaborately scripted

* G.C.D. O'Dell, *Shakespeare from Betterton to Irving* (New York, 1920), II, p. 464.

scenes of pageantry, *Henry VIII* peculiarly lent itself to opulent staging.

Both a radically changed view of English history and a twentieth-century reaction against the lavish, pictorial stagings of the Victorian era no doubt help to account for the play's relative neglect in modern times. Another important reason for the play's eclipse, however, has surely been the belief, originating in the late nineteenth century, that the play was written only in part by Shakespeare. There is no external evidence to support this view, yet perceived anomalies of style, diction, and poetic quality in the play prompted speculation that *Henry VIII* might have been coauthored by Shakespeare and one or more contemporary playwrights.

The Two Noble Kinsmen, for example, is ascribed on its title page to Shakespeare and John Fletcher, and Fletcher is also named in the Stationers' Register as Shakespeare's collaborator in a now lost play called *Cardenio*. Since Fletcher was Shakespeare's successor as principal dramatist for the King's Men, he remains the favored candidate for coauthorship of *Henry VIII*. Most critics and editors have found the coauthorship thesis convincing, although they have differed quite widely in their views about the respective contributions of Shakespeare, Fletcher, and possible others. Fletcher has been credited with the title *All Is True,* under which the play appears to have been first performed in 1613, yet the title under which the play was published, *The Famous History of the Life of King Henry the Eight[h],* has generally been credited to Shakespeare or the editors of the 1623 folio edition of his plays. (The folio text is the sole printed source for *Henry VIII*.)

Although the question of the play's authorship is an important and legitimate one, discussion of it has tended to preempt other critical concerns and exclude *Henry VIII* from consideration as an authentic Shakespearean play. The loss is ours. There is no escaping the fact that the play was included as Shakespeare's in the 1623 folio, edited by his fellow actors, who were in the best position to know. That ascription was never questioned, as I have said, before the late nineteenth century. In principle, *Henry VIII* must therefore count as a play by Shakespeare until decisively proven otherwise. To date, neither the intuitions of critics nor statistical analyses of the play's language and diction have disqualified it from full consideration within the Shakespearean canon. Indeed, the more systematically critics have tried to map the play's deviations from supposed Shakespearean norms, the more questionable those norms have come to seem, and the less capable of determining what is or is not definitively Shakespearean.

Even if coauthorship were proven, however, the fact wouldn't necessarily detract from the interest of the play or diminish Shakespeare's investment in it. Much recent criticism has shown that collaboration in the production of sixteenth- and seventeenth-century texts, especially play texts, was more normal than anomalous. The fact that a play carried a particular author's name never precluded revisions and additions by several "hands," and the actors, editors, and scribes who prepared the plays for the press contributed to the printed texts. The survival of so many plays by Shakespeare and his contemporaries in markedly different versions implies a lack of exclusive authorial control over the text (or its revisions) at any point in its publication history. Moreover, plays were the property of the acting companies, not of their named authors, and therefore not under the authors' control. Modern attachment to the imagined fact and value of sole, controlling authorship – the form of authorship still too often regarded as the very basis of literary merit or authenticity – is foreign to the world in which Shakespeare's plays were produced. There can be little doubt, however, that anachronistic devotion to the ideal of Shakespeare's sole authorship has hurt the fortunes of the supposedly collaborative *Henry VIII* in modern times.

Hardly less to be regretted, the coauthorship theory regarding *Henry VIII* has failed to live up to its own potential for generating interest in the play. Recent criticism has increasingly paid attention to Shakespeare's tendency, late in his playwriting career, to embrace coauthorship actively as an authorial mode. *Pericles, The Two Noble Kinsmen,* and the lost *Cardenio* were evidently coauthored by Shakespeare. To regard this coauthorship simply as evidence of Shakespeare's decline, semiretirement, or withdrawal from the full rigors of composition begs the question. As other critics have pointed out, this prejudicial view has been supported by the persistent myth that *The Tempest* (1611) was Shakespeare's last play, in which, as solo dramatist, he took his formal leave of the stage. Although that myth has negative consequences in general, it is particularly damaging to *Henry VIII*. That play was not only written after *The Tempest,* but has no less a claim to count as Shakespeare's last word.

Rather than diminishing the interest of *Henry VIII,* consideration of its possible coauthorship might in fact add to its interest; it could also expand our understanding of the last phase of Shakespeare's playwriting career. The avowed coauthorship of Francis Beaumont and John Fletcher, whose plays were very popular, gave a certain trendiness to coauthorship around the time *Henry VIII* was written. As the work of Jeffrey Masten among others has suggested, the avowed coauthorship of Beaumont and Fletcher, roughly coinciding with that of Shakespeare and Fletcher, provides a model for authorial bonding, interaction, and transference at odds with that of sole authorship. It is a model importantly at odds, what is more, with that of authorship as a phenomenon of male competition and compulsive self-assertion only. The point isn't that Shakespeare had no investment in his own authorship and no part in competitive authorial self-fashioning – his work gives ample evidence of both – but that collaboration was a phenomenon of the time that would clearly be embraced as an active option, even by Shakespeare.

Given that recent critiques of the sole-authorship fetish have now opened the way to renewed appreciation of *Henry VIII,* then, what features internal to the play might additionally explain its current neglect? Perhaps the most likely ones from the point of view of both staging and readership are, first, the play's reliance on reported rather than dramatically presented action; second, the play's relatively "transparent" rather than metaphorically dense language; third, the absence of larger-than-life entertainers like the Falstaff of *Henry IV,* Parts 1 and 2; and, last, a historical frame more restricted than the huge panoramic one of the history plays from *Richard II* through *Henry V* (or, indeed, from *Henry VI,* Parts 1, 2, and 3, through *Richard III*). The narrowing of the frame in *Henry VIII* coincides with a reduction in the sheer variety and exuberance of the earlier histories, and perhaps with a lowering of the dramatic intensity. Yet to regard *Henry VIII* as "lacking" on these counts is to refuse its specific dramaturgical challenges and achievements, including its possible critique of the earlier history plays. A Shakespeare who changes rather than repeats himself (or tries to repeat his earlier successes) is an interesting figure who calls for recognition in *Henry VIII.*

What, then, characterizes *Henry VIII* as the last of Shakespeare's English history plays, positioned as such in the folio immediately before the tragedies? What history does it relate, and how does it do so? The play is quite closely based on historical chronicles, mainly those of Raphael Holinshed (1587) and Edward Hall (1548). John Foxe's *Book of Martyrs* is a source for Act V. George Cavendish's *Negotiations of Cardinal Wolsey,* widely circulated in manuscript, though not published until 1641, may have been at least an indirect source. The play begins shortly after a celebrated peacemaking encounter in 1520 between Henry VIII and Francis I, King of France, in Picardy. This encounter took place on what came to be known as the Field of the Cloth of Gold, and was marked by elaborate displays and ceremonials, with each king seeking to outshine the other in opulent pageantry. Characteristically, this encounter is reported rather than witnessed in *Henry VIII,* and its effects prove short-lived. Both the emulous rivalry of the kings and traditional English xenophobia soon reassert themselves; the latter does so comically insofar as it turns out to be based on the fear that stylish French men are more sexually appealing to women than their English counterparts. Peace with France threatens to make Englishmen permanent losers in the arena of heterosexual competition.

All of this can hardly fail to recall both Shakespeare's *Henry V* and the long-standing national rivalry between the French and the English. Yet in *Henry VIII* that national rivalry, with its prospect of ever-renewed conflict, proves inconsequential. English domestic politics – the literally domestic politics of royal divorce and remarriage – soon take precedence. Neither historically nor in the play is Henry VIII destined to be another conquering English military leader on the model of Henry V. Nor will national destiny and identity remain closely tied to rivalry with France. *Henry VIII* thus actively revises a popular as well as apparently compelling nationalistic scenario of the earlier history plays.

Some readers of *Henry VIII* have, indeed, found it disappointing that the only pitched battle (a reported one at that) is fought with cudgels between porters and unruly, youthful revelers at the christening ceremonies for Elizabeth I at the end of the play, those revelers apparently belonging to something like modern youth gangs. Anticlimactic farce rather than heroic victory thus characterizes "warfare" in *Henry VIII;* perhaps the play is making a point about the exaggerated importance given to military action in both drama and history. Indeed, the marked distancing of action in *Henry VIII,* a feature that may make the play seem more neoclassically old-fashioned than Shakespeare's earlier history plays, is systematic.

That not only allows pageant and spectacle, scripted with unusual elaborateness in this play, to come to the fore, but implies that political spectacle, performance, and stage management are themselves the matter of history. Henry clearly gains command as king when he emerges from under the sway of Wolsey's eloquence and stage management, and begins to control both the language and staging of power himself. His mastery of Wolsey is manifested by the confidence with which he begins to deploy irony against him, after Wolsey has fatally betrayed his own double-dealing. Indeed, it is almost as if the overreaching Wolsey acts under a compulsion to undo himself, while Henry, like Prospero in *The Tempest* anticipating the propitious moment that delivers his enemies into his hands, awaits the pretext that will allow him to take control.

The narrative of *Henry VIII* is focused on some of the key personalities and events of Henry VIII's reign. Or, as Sir Henry Wotton said in a letter written in 1613, it "represent[s] some principal pieces of the reign of Henry 8." These include Henry himself as title character; the ambitious, conniving Cardinal Wolsey, Henry's Lord Chancellor when the play begins; Katherine of Aragon, the Spanish-born wife Henry divorces in order to marry Anne Bullen; Anne Bullen herself; the Duke of Buckingham, condemned to death for treason early in the play (Wolsey being widely held responsible for his fall); Stephen Gardiner, Bishop of Winchester and a defender of the Catholic faith already threatened by Protestant reform in England; and Thomas Cranmer, who becomes the Archbishop of Canterbury in the course of the play. The cast includes numerous secondary or minor characters, but ones of some significance even when they are only spectators of the pageants being staged by the great.

These are the main events of the play: Buckingham's execution; Henry's falling in love with Anne Bullen; the process through which Henry's marriage to Katherine gets annulled on the technical grounds that she had been lawfully wedded, in a consummated marriage, to his deceased elder brother Arthur (and thus that her subsequent marriage to Henry was incestuous under canon law); the fall of Wolsey and his replacement as Lord Chancellor by Sir Thomas More; the rise of Cranmer, already on his way to becoming the first English Protestant Archbishop of Canterbury; the birth of Anne's daughter Elizabeth, destined to rule as Queen of England; and, finally, the public festivities attending Elizabeth's christening, during which the "truth-telling" Cranmer prophesies her glorious reign to come.

As this summary indicates, the play very selectively covers some significant moments and personalities during the reign of Henry VIII. It omits a great deal from this reign, however, by ending with the birth of Elizabeth. Shakespeare's contemporaries would have known of the subsequent English break with the Catholic church, of Anne Bullen's execution on charges of treason and infidelity, of Thomas More's execution and replacement as Lord Chancellor by Thomas Cromwell, of Henry's four subsequent marriages, and of his death. Although the play is titled the "life" of Henry VIII, it stops far short of the end; in fact, it stops at the moment when Henry feels creatively reborn through the birth of his child – who, in one of the strangest moments of the play, is initially reported to him as a son – and thus like the paternal founder of a great nation rather than merely the inheritor of a kingdom. Unlike Katherine's daughter Mary, Elizabeth will apparently count as a son, and more. The rest lies beyond the frame of the play. Perhaps we are to understand that this residue has been rendered inconsequential, less by the birth of the miraculous Elizabeth, queen of the future, than by the presence on the throne, in 1613, of her male successor, James I.

Shakespeare's choosing to end the narrative at that point says much about his purposes in the play. The choice helps to explain, without explaining away, his omissions, chronological alterations, and contentious interpretations of the historical record even before the birth of Elizabeth in the play. (Many of these would have been as glaringly obvious to Shakespeare's contemporaries as they are to modern scholars.) In *Henry VIII,* as in all his history plays, Shakespeare's interest in English history is neither passive nor impartial. On the contrary, it is a strongly participatory, shaping interest in what we might now call the English national narrative: that is to say, the continuing story – or interwoven stories – of English national formation, mutating identity, and destiny. That interest was not Shakespeare's alone – indeed, for his plays to make sense to others, it could hardly have been his alone – but one capable of being shared with, and modified by, a host of collaborators, both on the stage and off. Concluding *Henry VIII* with the birth of Elizabeth orients the play toward the distant future rather than the concluding events of Henry's reign. The national destiny prophesied in the play, whether through Cranmer's visionary concluding speech or by implication elsewhere in the play, includes the foundation of a global empire: the play includes allusions to the wealth of the Indies and to English expansion into the New World through the Virginia colony. (Even racial mythology is already in the air as the play alludes to the New World Indian with his "great tool," V.3.32.)

Although Shakespeare was certainly not unaware of the provincialism and folly of aggressive English patriotism (a consciousness built into *Cymbeline,* for example), the production of large national narratives was one of the compelling projects of European political cultures as well as individual writers in Shakespeare's time. In that era of rapid national formation and assertion, there was no escaping the fact that the nation had become a principal unit of political and imaginative consciousness as well as of historical development. Shakespeare's part in scripting the English, Protestant, national narrative is clearly a major one, and *Henry VIII* contributes both distinctively and crucially to that enterprise.

In the context of that enterprise, the increasingly beleaguered Catholic power represented by Cardinal Wolsey in *Henry VIII* harks back to an earlier political epoch, one in which Western Europe could conceive of itself as the Holy Roman Empire, a unitary political entity under the spiritual command of Rome. We hear during the play that Wolsey had hoped to become Bishop of Toledo in Spain; he has no national attachment, and can hope to pursue his ambitions anywhere in Europe. The fall of Wolsey in *Henry VIII* thus represents the passing of an ancient political era, "catholic" in both senses of the term. In the course of the play, the independence of the English kingdom and the subordination of religious to national, political authority become increasingly entrenched; by the same token, Henry is increasingly "liberated" from Wolsey's arrogant domination and attempted manipulation. Although the strong-minded Katherine is almost hagiographically presented in the play as a model spouse and Christian woman, she nevertheless remains, even in her own mind, a Spanish "stranger." When Wolsey sees the divorce coming, he plans to marry Henry off to the sister of the French king (historically, Marguerite of Navarre, author of the *Heptaméron*), but before he can act, Henry has already married Anne on his own initiative. She, in contrast to the foreigners, is definitively an English beauty with childbearing potential. Indeed, unlike Katherine, who offers the king political advice, Anne is little more than a woman whose potentially disruptive sexuality will be conscripted for dynastic purposes. Marriage legitimizes formerly illicit relations between Henry and Anne, just as christening sanctifies the offspring of that union. Significantly, the threat of both political and sexual "disorder," including miscegenation, reappears at the moment of the christening through the comically indignant perceptions of the porter:

What should you do but knock 'em down by th'
dozens? Is this Moorfields to muster in? Or have we
some strange Indian with the great tool come to
court, the women so besiege us? Bless me, what a
fry of fornication is at door! On my Christian conscience this one christening will beget a thousand;
here will be father, godfather, and all together.

(V.3.30-36)

The porter's vision of social upheaval conflates women's supposedly inordinate sexual appetites with plebeian riot and lust for colonial natives. Not only does the distinction between natural and spiritual paternity (father/god-father) collapse, but reproduction runs out of control in a prolific begetting of anonymous thousands. In marked contrast, the birth and christening of Elizabeth represent controlled, economical, purposeful reproduction in the service of political order and national propagation. The threat of disorder surfaces only to be dispelled. What will henceforth be reproduced in England is pure Englishness, a fact at least as consequential as political rivalry with other European nations.

Spectators in the play report that Anne has been ex-posed to public view during the coronation ceremonies. We hear that her beauty elicited thrilled public comment and approval for the remarriage. This display may strike us as a distasteful form of publicity, she being put onstage as a politically exploitable object of desire and perhaps as Henry's new trophy wife. Yet she is also being displayed as the mother of Elizabeth, thus underlining the crucial importance of reproduction and succession to the shaping of a national destiny. Moreover, the birth of Elizabeth, even though she is not the wished-for son, enables Henry to feel empowered both as a man and a king, especially after

Cranmer has framed the event to Henry's liking. Not even Elizabeth's famed virginity, also prophesied by Cranmer, will interrupt this royal succession, since Cranmer's prophecy includes the "miracle" by which James I, not a biological heir, will succeed Elizabeth:

> as when
> The bird of wonder dies, the maiden phoenix,
> Her ashes new create another heir
> As great in admiration as herself,
> So shall she leave her blessedness to one
> (When heaven shall call her from this cloud
>   of darkness)
> Who from the sacred ashes of her honor
> Shall starlike rise, as great in fame as she was,
> And so stand fixed.
>   (V.4.39–47)

Critics have often noted that *Henry VIII* shares many traits with Shakespeare's late "romances" (*Pericles, Cymbeline, A Winter's Tale*). The motifs of miraculous birth or recovery of a daughter, of adult rebirth of the king, of verified prophecy, and of a providential outcome to the seemingly incalculable vicissitudes and manifold corruptions of history are among the "romance" elements of *Henry VIII*. In this play, however, such romance motifs remain at the service of the national narrative. They not only contribute to the narrative but draw attention to its necessarily imaginative, fictionalized, and inspirational character – or, to put it more negatively, its bondage to fantasy and wish fulfillment rather than historical veracity. The play's alternative title, *All Is True,* can thus be read as mordantly ironic: "all is false" would make equal sense, a fact that wouldn't necessarily have escaped some of Shakespeare's contemporaries. Yet that wholly ironic reading is historically implausible, and in any case the title *All Is True* preempts distinctions between truth and falsity,

history and fiction, that might be applied to the play. Undoing such distinctions as a source, not of ethical choice
but of sterile contention and anxiety, forms a large part of
Shakespeare's late "romance" agenda. So does the inculca-
tion of belief that truth does or will prevail everywhere.
The appearance of falsity is thus either immaterial or ulti-
mately another manifestation of truth: such is the leap of
faith for which romance calls upon us.

The national destiny Cranmer prophesies at Elizabeth's
christening links the historical past to the present in
which the play was being written and performed. It is a
prophecy that anticipates the full course of Elizabeth's
reign and the succession of James I; it has therefore already been "verified" in large measure by the time of the
play's performance in 1613. Shakespearean hindsight, in
other words, informs the prophecy spoken by Cranmer in
Henry VIII.

Critics seeking to explain why *Henry VIII* was particularly timely in 1613 have suggested that the play was intended to "recall" James I to the historic destiny of which
he was the principal bearer, and to re-instill in him an
elevated vision of his kingship, compromised as it had become by political corruption, vacillation, and mismanage-
ment. It has convincingly been argued, in any event, that
Henry VIII alludes directly to the marriage of James I's
daughter Elizabeth to Prince Frederick, Elector Palatine
and leader of German Protestants, on February 14, 1613.
Shakespeare and others may well have seen that event as a
timely reassertion of national, Protestant values and English leadership – James was often suspected of being soft
on Catholicism – in which, at the same time, the glories
of the first Elizabeth were being recalled. Jacobean nostal-
gia for Elizabeth I has been well documented by critics; a
1613 play ending with the *birth* of Elizabeth certainly at-
tests to the continuing hold on the imagination of the late
queen, exceeding that of her "famous" father.

The play's representation of Henry VIII's reign, then,

including its emphases and omissions, appears largely determined by the exigencies of the national narrative. That narrative is, in turn, being constructed in ways that differ significantly from those of the earlier history plays. What *Henry VIII* apparently offered contemporary English audiences was a revision and updating of the national narrative, emphasizing the "miracle" of royal succession, into which they could incorporate themselves. That some, perhaps many, chose to do so seems likely (that is one possible explanation for the play's apparently good reception in the theater), but the play certainly leaves room for reservations and even dissenting views. Strong polarization and communal fragmentation are thereby avoided. As previously mentioned, the play's "losers" – Buckingham, Wolsey, and, above all, Katherine – have prevailed in the play's stage history as its most engaging characters in performance; their great, concluding set pieces have often been excerpted from the play for theatrical recital. None of these characters is demonized as an antagonist of the national destiny. Hatred for Wolsey in the play seems generally based on the envious resentment and class disdain of the aristocracy, while not even Henry has a word to say against Katherine, even though he plans to divorce her. All these characters leave the stage with dignity, their "fall" from greatness being staged with some of the stylized, ceremonious formality and pathos of medieval tragedy. (As is the case with the play's reporting of action, an "old-fashioned" dramaturgy is being linked here to a contemporary purpose – namely, that of allowing those overtaken by history to depart at peace, without threatening to return and haunt the living.) The pageant staged at the death of Katherine, which she sees as a heavenly vision, belongs to a different genre from the pageants so lavishly orchestrated in the service of power by Wolsey and the king: she inhabits a different order from the one they inhabit. The frame of this play, like those of the Shakespearean romances, can evidently accommodate incommensurable realities. Perhaps that is another implication of the title *All Is True*.

To conclude, then, *Henry VIII* is a play that eminently deserves full recognition within the Shakespearean canon. Discussion either of the history plays or of Shakespeare's national vision that slights *Henry VIII* is unquestionably deficient. Moreover, we may hope that the merits of the play will increasingly vie for interest with the best-known historical fact about it: during one of its performances in 1613, the Globe theater burned down, its thatched roof having caught fire after a discharge of cannons (the cannons probably having been those fired to announce the arrival of the king and his party at Wolsey's banquet in Act I, scene 4). That event, colorfully reported in the 1613 letter by Sir Henry Wotton already cited, has done more than anything else to etch the play in modern consciousness, but repetition of the story sometimes conveys the implication that only an unusual accident lends interest to *Henry VIII*. The play deserves far better than that.

JONATHAN CREWE
Dartmouth College

Note on the Text

HENRY VIII WAS first printed in the 1623 folio volume of Shakespeare's plays. It appears as the last of the English history plays, immediately before the tragedies. The text is carefully printed, and relatively free of apparent errors and anomalies. Unlike some previous modern editions, this one fully adheres to the folio act and scene divisions. The spelling of names has been regularized, and inconsistencies in the speech prefixes have been resolved. I have incorporated a substantial number of glosses from the earlier Pelican text edited by F. David Hoeniger. Substantive departures from the folio are listed below, with the adopted reading in italics followed by the folio reading in roman.

I.1 42–47 *All . . . together* (assigned to Buckingham in F)   63 *web, a* Web. O   69–70 *that? / . . . hell the* that, / . . . Hell? The   79–80 *council out, / . . . in he* Councell, out / . . . in, he   96 *Bordeaux* Burdeux   120 *venom-mouthed* venom'd-mouth'd   123 *chafed* chaff'd   200 *Hereford* Hertford   219 *Perk* Pecke; *chancellor* Councellour

I.2 67 *business* basenesse   156 *feared* feare   164 *confession's* Commissions   180 *To* For this· to   190 *Bulmer* Blumer   191 *time. Being* time, being

I.3 59 *wherewithal. In him* wherewithall in him;

II.1 20 *Perk* Pecke   86 *mark* make

II.3 14 *quarrel, fortune, do* quarrel. Fortune, do   32 *cheveril* Chiverell   59 *note's* notes   61 *of you, and* of you, to you; and

II.4 131 *Exeunt* Exit   172 *A* And   197 *throe* throw   217 *summons. Unsolicited* Summons unsolicited

III.1 23 s.d. *Campeius* Campian   61 *your* our   83 *profit. Can* profit can   124 *accursed* a curse

III.2 142 *glad* gald   233 *commission, lords?* Commission? Lords,   343 *Chattels* Castels

IV.1 20 SECOND GENTLEMAN   34 *Kimbolton* Kymmalton   36 s.d., item 4 *Choristers* Quirristers   54–56 SECOND GENTLEMAN *Their . . . / FIRST GENTLEMAN And . . . SECOND GENTLEMAN No . . . / FIRST GENTLEMAN God . . .* 2 Their . . . / And . . . 2 No . . . / 1 God . . .   78 *press* prease   101 *Stokely* Stokesly

IV.2 7 *think* thank   82 **s.d.** *reverent* reverend
V.1 37 *time* Lime   55 *Exeunt* Exit   139 *precipice* Precepit
V.2 8 *piece* Peere   120, 122 CHANCELLOR Cham.   207 *brother love*
    Brother; loue
V.3 81 *press* praesse
V.4 37 *ways* way

The Life of King Henry
the Eighth

[Names of the Actors

KING HENRY THE EIGHTH
CARDINAL WOLSEY
CARDINAL CAMPEIUS
CAPUCHIUS, *ambassador from the Emperor Charles V*
CRANMER, *Archbishop of Canterbury*
DUKE OF NORFOLK
DUKE OF BUCKINGHAM
DUKE OF SUFFOLK
EARL OF SURREY
LORD CHAMBERLAIN
LORD CHANCELLOR
GARDINER, *King Henry's secretary, afterward Bishop of Winchester*
BISHOP OF LINCOLN
LORD ABERGAVENNY
LORD SANDYS *(Sir Walter Sandys)*
SIR HENRY GUILFORD
SIR THOMAS LOVELL
SIR ANTHONY DENNY
SIR NICHOLAS VAUX
BRANDON*
CROMWELL, *servant to Wolsey*
GRIFFITH, *gentleman usher to Queen Katherine*
THREE GENTLEMEN
DOCTOR BUTTS, *physician to the King*
GARTER KING-OF-ARMS

* *Brandon* (perhaps identical with the Duke of Suffolk above, whose name was Charles Brandon)

SURVEYOR TO THE DUKE OF BUCKINGHAM
DOORKEEPER OF THE COUNCIL CHAMBER
SERGEANT AT ARMS
PORTER, AND HIS MAN
PAGE TO GARDINER
SECRETARIES TO WOLSEY
A CRIER
QUEEN KATHERINE, *wife to King Henry, afterward divorced*
ANNE BULLEN, *her Maid of Honor, afterward Queen*
OLD LADY, *friend to Anne Bullen*
PATIENCE, *woman to Queen Katherine*
SPIRITS
LORDS, LADIES, BISHOPS, JUDGES, GENTLEMEN, AND PRIESTS; LORD MAYOR OF LONDON AND ALDERMEN; VERGERS, SCRIBES, GUARDS, ATTENDANTS, SERVANTS, AND COMMON PEOPLE; WOMEN ATTENDING UPON QUEEN KATHERINE

SCENE: *London; Kimbolton*]
*

The Life of King Henry
the Eighth

THE PROLOGUE

ꙮ **Pro.**

I come no more to make you laugh. Things now
That bear a weighty and a serious brow,
Sad, high, and working, full of state and woe,   3
Such noble scenes as draw the eye to flow
We now present. Those that can pity, here
May (if they think it well) let fall a tear:
The subject will deserve it. Such as give
Their money out of hope they may believe,
May here find truth too. Those that come to see
Only a show or two and so agree   10
The play may pass – if they be still and willing,
I'll undertake may see away their shilling   12
Richly in two short hours. Only they   13
That come to hear a merry bawdy play,   14

Prologue 3 *Sad . . . working* serious, lofty, and moving; *state* stateliness,
high matters 10 *show* scene 12 *shilling* coin paid for an expensive seat
close to the stage 13 *two . . . hours* (a round number, not the exact running
time of *Henry VIII*) 14 *merry . . . play.*(possible allusion to an earlier Henry
VIII play by William Rowley [1605], which included clowns and onstage
fighting)

15 A noise of targets, or to see a fellow
16 In a long motley coat guarded with yellow,
17 Will be deceived. For, gentle hearers, know
   To rank our chosen truth with such a show
19 As fool and fight is, beside forfeiting
20 Our own brains and the opinion that we bring
21 To make that only true we now intend,
22 Will leave us never an understanding friend.
   Therefore, for goodness' sake, and as you are known
24 The first and happiest hearers of the town,
25 Be sad, as we would make ye. Think ye see
   The very persons of our noble story
   As they were living. Think you see them great,
   And followed with the general throng and sweat
   Of thousand friends. Then, in a moment, see
30 How soon this mightiness meets misery.
   And if you can be merry then, I'll say
   A man may weep upon his wedding day.

                              *

   ∾ **I.1** *Enter the Duke of Norfolk at one door; at*
      the other, the Duke of Buckingham and the Lord
      Abergavenny.

BUCKINGHAM
   Good morrow and well met. How have ye done
   Since last we saw in France?

---

15 *targets* shields (here, being struck)   16 *motley coat* particolored garb of a
jester; *guarded* trimmed   17 *deceived* disappointed   19–20 *forfeiting . . .*
brains (1) abandoning all claims to intelligence, (2) squandering our intellec-
tual effort   20 *opinion* intent, disposition   21 *make . . . intend* i.e., make
the work we propose true to the historical facts   22 *understanding* (play on
"understanders," the "groundlings" who, for lower admission prices, watched
the play standing around the stage)   24 *happiest* most fortunate   25 *sad* serious
   I.1 London, the royal palace

NORFOLK   I thank your grace,
  Healthful, and ever since a fresh admirer   3
  Of what I saw there.   4
BUCKINGHAM   An untimely ague
  Stayed me a prisoner in my chamber when
  Those suns of glory, those two lights of men,   6
  Met in the vale of Andren.   7
NORFOLK   'Twixt Guynes and Arde.
  I was then present, saw them salute on horseback,
  Beheld them when they lighted, how they clung   9
  In their embracement, as they grew together;   10
  Which had they, what four throned ones could have   11
    weighed
  Such a compounded one?
BUCKINGHAM   All the whole time
  I was my chamber's prisoner.
NORFOLK   Then you lost
  The view of earthly glory. Men might say
  Till this time pomp was single, but now married   15
  To one above itself. Each following day
  Became the next day's master, till the last   17
  Made former wonders, its. Today the French,   18
  All clinquant, all in gold, like heathen gods   19
  Shone down the English; and tomorrow they   20
  Made Britain India: every man that stood   21
  Showed like a mine. Their dwarfish pages were   22
  As cherubins, all gilt. The madams too,   23
  Not used to toil, did almost sweat to bear

---

3 *fresh* undimmed 4 *ague* fever 6 *Those . . . men* i.e., Henry VIII and
Francis I of France 7 *Guynes . . . Arde* i.e., Guines and Ardres, in Picardy
9 *lighted* alighted 10 *as* as if 11 *weighed* equaled in weight 15–16
pomp . . . itself i.e., the united pomp of the two kings took pomp itself to a
higher level, as if it had married up 17 *master* teacher 18 *Made . . . its* ab-
sorbed all the glories of the previous days 19 *clinquant* glittering 21 *India*
i.e., the West Indies 22 *Showed* appeared 23 *madams* ladies of rank

25   The pride upon them, that their very labor
26   Was to them as a painting. Now this masque
27   Was cried incomparable; and th' ensuing night
    Made it a fool and beggar. The two kings,
    Equal in luster, were now best, now worst,
30   As presence did present them: him in eye
    Still him in praise; and being present both,
32   'Twas said they saw but one, and no discerner
33   Durst wag his tongue in censure. When these suns
34   (For so they phrase 'em) by their heralds challenged
    The noble spirits to arms, they did perform·
36   Beyond thought's compass, that former fabulous story,
    Being now seen possible enough, got credit,
38   That Bevis was believed.

BUCKINGHAM   O you go far.

NORFOLK
39   As I belong to worship and affect
40   In honor honesty, the tract of ev'ry thing
41   Would by a good discourser lose some life
    Which action's self was tongue to. All was royal.
43   To the disposing of it nought rebelled;
44   Order gave each thing view. The office did
    Distinctly his full function. Who did guide,
    I mean who set the body and the limbs
47   Of this great sport together? As you guess:
48   One, certes, that promises no element

---

25 *pride* splendid attire   26 *Was ... painting* i.e., made them flush as if they were wearing cosmetics; *masque* pageant   27 *cried* proclaimed   30–31 *him ... praise* the one in view was the one praised   32 *saw ... one* i.e., both appeared alike in majesty; *discerner* onlooker   33 *censure* judgment   34 *phrase* call   36 *that* so that   38 *Bevis* Bevis of Southampton (a legendary hero of ballads and romances)   39 *worship* nobility   39–40 *affect ... honesty* love and pursue truth for my honor   40 *tract* course   41–42 *Would ... to* i.e., the action spoke for itself more eloquently than even a good storyteller could convey   43 *disposing* arrangement   44–45 *The office ... function* each official performed his role perfectly   47 *sport* entertainment   48 *certes* certainly; *promises no element* i.e., you wouldn't expect to be taking part

In such a business.
BUCKINGHAM   I pray you who, my lord?
NORFOLK
  All this was ordered by the good discretion   50
  Of the right reverend Cardinal of York.   51
BUCKINGHAM
  The devil speed him! No man's pie is freed
  From his ambitious finger. What had he
  To do in these fierce vanities? I wonder   54
  That such a keech can with his very bulk   55
  Take up the rays o' th' beneficial sun   56
  And keep it from the earth.
NORFOLK   Surely, sir,
  There's in him stuff that puts him to these ends;
  For, being not propped by ancestry, whose grace
  Chalks successors their way, nor called upon   60
  For high feats done to th' crown, neither allied   61
  To eminent assistants, but spiderlike   62
  Out of his self-drawing web, a gives us note,   63
  The force of his own merit makes his way,   64
  A gift that heaven gives for him, which buys   65
  A place next to the king.
ABERGAVENNY   I cannot tell
  What heaven hath given him. Let some graver eye
  Pierce into that; but I can see his pride
  Peep through each part of him. Whence has he that?
  If not from hell the devil is a niggard,   70
  Or has given all before, and he begins   71

---

51 *Cardinal of York* i.e., Cardinal Wolsey, who had been born a butcher's
son, and was not a member of the nobility   54 *fierce vanities* (1) extravagant
shows, (2) entertainments of the aggressively powerful and ambitious   55
keech lump of fat   56 *Take up* block out; *sun* i.e., the king   60 *Chalks* marks
out   61 *to th' crown* for king and country   62 *assistants* (1) public officials,
(2) powerful associates   63 *self-drawing* spun out of himself; *a . . . note* he
lets it be known   64 *makes his way* wins advancement   65 *for him* on his be-
half   70 *niggard* grudging hoarder   71–72 *he begins . . . himself* i.e., the
devil having given him all his pride, Wolsey has begun a new hell himself

A new hell in himself.

BUCKINGHAM   Why the devil,

73   Upon this French going out, took he upon him
74   (Without the privity o' th' king) t' appoint
75   Who should attend on him? He makes up the file
      Of all the gentry, for the most part such
77   To whom as great a charge as little honor
78   He meant to lay upon; and his own letter,
      The honorable board of council out,
80   Must fetch him in he papers.

ABERGAVENNY   I do know
      Kinsmen of mine, three at the least, that have
82   By this so sickened their estates that never
      They shall abound as formerly.

BUCKINGHAM   O many
84   Have broke their backs with laying manors on 'em
      For this great journey. What did this vanity
86   But minister communication of
      A most poor issue?

NORFOLK   Grievingly I think
88   The peace between the French and us not values
      The cost that did conclude it.

BUCKINGHAM   Every man,
90   After the hideous storm that followed, was
91   A thing inspired, and not consulting broke
      Into a general prophecy: that this tempest,
93   Dashing the garment of this peace, aboded

---

73 *going out* expedition   74 *the privity* making the king privy to his inten-
tions   75 *file* list   77–78 *To whom . . . upon* i.e., whom he meant to tax rather
than honor   78–80 *his . . . papers* i.e., he may summon ("paper") whomever
he wishes without consulting the council   82 *sickened* impoverished   84
Have . . . 'em i.e., have ruined themselves by spending whole manors' worth
on their wardrobes   86 *minister communication* give occasion for talk   88
not values isn't worth   90 *the hideous storm* (an actual storm that, according
to the chroniclers, interrupted the proceedings on June 18)   91 *thing inspired* prophet   91–92 *not consulting . . . prophecy* i.e., was taken as a
prophecy even without any consultation   93 *aboded* boded

The sudden breach on't.   94
NORFOLK   Which is budded out;
For France hath flawed the league and hath attached   95
Our merchants' goods at Bordeaux.
ABERGAVENNY   Is it therefore
Th' ambassador is silenced?   97
NORFOLK   Marry is't!
ABERGAVENNY
A proper title of a peace, and purchased   98
At a superfluous rate!   99
BUCKINGHAM   Why, all this business
Our reverend cardinal carried.   100
NORFOLK   Like it your grace,
The state takes notice of the private difference   101
Betwixt you and the cardinal. I advise you
(And take it from a heart that wishes towards you
Honor and plenteous safety) that you read   104
The cardinal's malice and his potency
Together; to consider further, that
What his high hatred would effect wants not   107
A minister in his power. You know his nature,   108
That he's revengeful; and I know his sword
Hath a sharp edge; it's long, and 't may be said   *110*
It reaches far, and where 'twill not extend
Thither he darts it. Bosom up my counsel;   112
You'll find it wholesome. Lo where comes that rock

---

94 *sudden . . . on't* imminent breach of the peace   95 *flawed* broken; *attached* seized   97 *silenced* i.e., the French ambassador has been confined to his quarters (reported in Hall's chronicle); *Marry* (an exclamation – a mild oath, originally on the name of the Virgin Mary)   98 *A . . . peace* A fine thing to call a peace!   99 *superfluous* extravagant   100 *Like it* if it please   101 *difference* quarrel   104 *read* consider   107 *wants not* doesn't lack   108 *minister* agent   112 *darts it* i.e., shoots an arrow; *Bosom up* hide in your bosom

114   That I advise your shunning.
        Enter Cardinal Wolsey, the purse borne before him,
        certain of the Guard, and two Secretaries with papers.
        The Cardinal in his passage fixeth his eye on
        Buckingham, and Buckingham on him, both full
        of disdain.

        WOLSEY
115   The Duke of Buckingham's surveyor, ha?
116   Where's his examination?
        FIRST SECRETARY   Here, so please you.
        WOLSEY
        Is he in person ready?
        FIRST SECRETARY   Ay, please your grace.
        WOLSEY
        Well, we shall then know more, and Buckingham
119   Shall lessen this big look. *Exeunt Cardinal and his train.*
        BUCKINGHAM
120   This butcher's cur is venom-mouthed, and I
        Have not the power to muzzle him; therefore best
122   Not wake him in his slumber. A beggar's book
123   Outworths a noble's blood.
        NORFOLK   What, are you chafed?
124   Ask God for temp'rance. That's th' appliance only
        Which your disease requires.
        BUCKINGHAM   I read in's looks
        Matter against me, and his eye reviled
        Me as his abject object. At this instant
128   He bores me with some trick. He's gone to th' king.
        I'll follow and outstare him.
        NORFOLK   Stay, my lord,
130   And let your reason with your choler question
        What 'tis you go about. To climb steep hills

---

114 s.d. *purse* bag containing the great seal, emblem of the Lord Chancellor's office 115 *surveyor* estate overseer 116 *examination* paper containing the witness's deposition 119 *big look* haughty expression 122 *book* learning 123 *chafed* angered 124 *appliance* remedy 128 *bores* cheats 130 *choler* rage

Requires slow pace at first. Anger is like
A full hot horse, who being allowed his way,
Self-mettle tires him. Not a man in England   134
Can advise me like you. Be to yourself
As you would to your friend.
BUCKINGHAM   I'll to the king
And from a mouth of honor quite cry down
This Ipswich fellow's insolence, or proclaim   138
There's difference in no persons.   139
NORFOLK   Be advised.
Heat not a furnace for your foe so hot   140
That it do singe yourself. We may outrun
By violent swiftness that which we run at,
And lose by overrunning. Know you not
The fire that mounts the liquor till't run o'er   144
In seeming to augment it wastes it? Be advised.
I say again there is no English soul
More stronger to direct you than yourself,
If with the sap of reason you would quench,
Or but allay the fire of passion.   149
BUCKINGHAM   Sir,
I am thankful to you, and I'll go along   150
By your prescription. But this top-proud fellow –   151
Whom from the flow of gall I name not, but   152
From sincere motions – by intelligence,   153
And proofs as clear as founts in July when
We see each grain of gravel, I do know
To be corrupt and treasonous.
NORFOLK   Say not treasonous.
BUCKINGHAM
To th' king I'll say't and make my vouch as strong   157

---

134 *Self-mettle* his own ardor   138 *Ipswich* (Wolsey's humble birthplace, a
village in the London orbit)   139 *There's difference . . . no persons* differences
of rank don't exist; *Be advised* take care   144 *mounts the liquor* causes the
fluid to rise   149 *allay* temper   151 *prescription* advice   152–53 *Whom . . .
motions* whom I mention, not out of anger, but with sincere motives   153
intelligence secret information   157 *vouch* attestation

As shore of rock. Attend. This holy fox,
Or wolf, or both (for he is equal rav'nous
160   As he is subtile, and as prone to mischief
161   As able to perform't), his mind and place
Infecting one another, yea reciprocally,
Only to show his pomp as well in France
164   As here at home, suggests the king our master
To this last costly treaty; th' interview
That swallowed so much treasure and like a glass
167   Did break i' th' wrenching.

NORFOLK   Faith, and so it did.

BUCKINGHAM
Pray give me favor, sir. This cunning cardinal
169   The articles o' th' combination drew
170   As himself pleased; and they were ratified
As he cried "Thus let be," to as much end
172   As give a crutch to th' dead. But our count-cardinal
Has done this, and 'tis well; for worthy Wolsey
(Who cannot err) he did it. Now this follows
(Which, as I take it, is a kind of puppy
176   To th' old dam, treason), Charles the emperor,
Under pretense to see the queen his aunt
178   (For 'twas indeed his color, but he came
To whisper Wolsey), here makes visitation.
180   His fears were that the interview betwixt
England and France might through their amity
182   Breed him some prejudice, for from this league
Peeped harms that menaced him: privily
184   Deals with our cardinal, and, as I trow,
Which I do well; for I am sure the emperor
Paid ere he promised, whereby his suit was granted
Ere it was asked; but when the way was made,

---

161 *place* office   164 *suggests* inveigles, prompts   167 *wrenching* (1) rinsing,
(2) rough handling   169 *combination* pact   172 *count-cardinal* i.e., upstart
cardinal behaving like a nobleman   176 *dam* mother (i.e., of the *puppy*)
178 *color* pretext   182 *Breed . . . prejudice* work to his disadvantage   184
trow believe

And paved with gold, the emperor thus desired,
That he would please to alter the king's course
And break the foresaid peace. Let the king know   *190*
(As soon he shall by me) that thus the cardinal
Does buy and sell his honor as he pleases,
And for his own advantage.
NORFOLK   I am sorry
To hear this of him, and could wish he were
Something mistaken in't.   *195*
BUCKINGHAM   No, not a syllable.
I do pronounce him in that very shape   *196*
He shall appear in proof.   *197*
      Enter Brandon, a Sergeant at Arms before him, and
      two or three of the Guard.
BRANDON
Your office, sergeant; execute it.
SERGEANT   Sir,
My lord the Duke of Buckingham, and Earl
Of Hereford, Stafford, and Northampton, I   *200*
Arrest thee of high treason, in the name
Of our most sovereign king.   *202*
BUCKINGHAM   Lo you, my lord,
The net has fall'n upon me! I shall perish
Under device and practice.   *204*
BRANDON   I am sorry
To see you ta'en from liberty, to look on   *205*
The business present. 'Tis his highness' pleasure
You shall to th' Tower.
BUCKINGHAM   It will help me nothing
To plead mine innocence, for that dye is on me
Which makes my whit'st part black. The will of heav'n
Be done in this and all things! I obey.   *210*
O my Lord Aberga'ny, fare you well!

---

195 *Something mistaken* somewhat misperceived **196** *pronounce* make
known **197** *in proof* (1) in experience, (2) when exposed **202** *Lo* look
204 *device and practice* stratagem and plot   **205** *look on* be a witness of

BRANDON
    Nay, he must bear you company.
        [To Abergavenny]   The king
    Is pleased you shall to th' Tower till you know
    How he determines further.
ABERGAVENNY   .   As the duke said,
    The will of heaven bè done, and the king's pleasure
    By me obeyed!
BRANDON   Here is a warrant from
217 The king t' attach Lord Montacute and the bodies
    Of the duke's confessor, John de la Car,
    One Gilbert Perk, his chancellor –
BUCKINGHAM   So, so!
220 These are the limbs o' th' plot. No more, I hope.   ₁
BRANDON
    A monk o' th' Chartreux.
BUCKINGHAM   O, Michael Hopkins?
BRANDON   He.
BUCKINGHAM   .
    My surveyor is false. The o'ergreat cardinal
223 Hath showed him gold; my life is spanned already.
    I am the shadow of poor Buckingham,
225 Whose figure even this instant cloud puts on
    By dark'ning my clear sun. My lord, farewell.   *Exeunt.*
                        ✳

    ✑ I.2 *Cornets. Enter King Henry, leaning on the Cardi-*
            nal's shoulder, the Nobles, [the Cardinal's Secretary,]
            and Sir Thomas Lovell. The Cardinal places himself
            under the King's feet on his right side.

KING
  1   My life itself, and the best heart of it,

---

217 *attach* arrest   **223** *spanned* measured out   **225** *cloud puts on* is becoming clouded
    I.2 The council chamber   **1** *best heart* very essence

Thanks you for this great care. I stood i' th' level   2
Of a full-charged confederacy, and give thanks   3
To you that choked it. Let be called before us
That gentleman of Buckingham's; in person
I'll hear him his confessions justify,   6
And point by point the treasons of his master
He shall again relate.   8
> *A noise within, crying "Room for the Queen!" Enter*
> *the Queen, ushered by the Duke of Norfolk, and*
> *Suffolk. She kneels. [The] King riseth from his state,*
> *takes her up, kisses and placeth her by him.*

KATHERINE
Nay, we must longer kneel. I am a suitor.

KING
Arise and take place by us. Half your suit   *10*
Never name to us; you have half our power.
The other moiety ere you ask is given.   12
Repeat your will, and take it.   13

KATHERINE   Thank your majesty.
That you would love yourself, and in that love
Not unconsidered leave your honor nor
The dignity of your office, is the point
Of my petition.

KING   Lady mine, proceed.

KATHERINE
I am solicited, not by a few,
And those of true condition, that your subjects   19
Are in great grievance. There have been commissions   20
Sent down among 'em, which hath flawed the heart   21
Of all their loyalties; wherein, although,
My good lord cardinal, they vent reproaches
Most bitterly on you as putter-on

---

2 *level* line of fire   3 *full-charged* fully loaded; *confederacy* conspiracy   6 *jus-*
tify confirm   8 s.d. *state* throne   12 *moiety* portion   13 *Repeat* state   19
true condition loyal disposition   20 *grievance* distress; *commissions* tax writs
21 *flawed* broken

Of these exactions, yet the king our master –
26 Whose honor heaven shield from soil! – even he es-
capes not
27 Language unmannerly; yea such which breaks
The sides of loyalty and almost appears
In loud rebellion.

NORFOLK   Not almost appears –
30 It doth appear. For upon these taxations,
The clothiers all not able to maintain
32 The many to them longing, have put off
33 The spinsters, carders, fullers, weavers, who,
Unfit for other life, compelled by hunger
And lack of other means, in desperate manner
36 Daring th' event to th' teeth, are all in uproar,
37 And danger serves among them.

KING   Taxation?
Wherein? And what taxation? My lord cardinal,
You that are blamed for it alike with us,
40 Know you of this taxation?

WOLSEY   Please you, sir,
41 I know but of a single part in aught
42 Pertains to th' state, and front but in that file
43 Where others tell steps with me.

KATHERINE   No, my lord?
44 You know no more than others? But you frame
45 Things that are known alike, which are not wholesome
46 To those which would not know them and yet must
47 Perforce be their acquaintance. These exactions

---

26 *soil* taint   27–28 *breaks / The sides* ruptures the bounds   32 *longing* belonging (i.e., employees dependent upon them)   33 *spinsters* spinners;
carders those who comb the wool for impurities; *fullers* those who beat the
wool to clean and mat it   36 *Daring . . . to th' teeth* i.e., defiantly accepting
the risks of revolt   37 *danger . . . among them* i.e., they accept danger but
also threaten mischief   41 *a single part* one person's share   42 *front . . . file*
march in the front rank   43 *tell steps* march in step   44 *frame* shape, insti-
gate   45 *known alike* known to all (in council)   46 *would not know* don't
want to know   47 *exactions* onerous requirements

(Whereof my sovereign would have note) they are   48
Most pestilent to th' hearing; and, to bear 'em,
The back is sacrifice to th' load. They say   50
They are devised by you, or else you suffer
Too hard an exclamation.   52
KING   Still exaction!
The nature of it? In what kind, let's know,   53
Is this exaction?
KATHERINE   I am much too venturous
In tempting of your patience, but am boldened
Under your promised pardon. The subject's grief   56
Comes through commissions, which compels from each
The sixth part of his substance, to be levied
Without delay; and the pretense for this
Is named, your wars in France. This makes bold   60
  mouths.
Tongues spit their duties out, and cold hearts freeze
Allegiance in them. Their curses now
Live where their prayers did; and it's come to pass
This tractable obedience is a slave   64
To each incensèd will. I would your highness   65
Would give it quick consideration, for
There is no primer business.   67
KING   By my life,
This is against our pleasure.
WOLSEY   And for me,
I have no further gone in this than by
A single voice, and that not passed me but   70
By learned approbation of the judges. If I am
Traduced by ignorant tongues, which neither know   72
My faculties nor person yet will be   73

---

48 *note* knowledge   50 *is sacrifice* becomes a sacrifice   52 *exclamation* outcry, reproach   53 *kind* form   56 *grief* grievance   64 *tractable* docile   65 *each incensèd will* each individual's outraged passion   67 *primer* more urgent   70 *single voice* unanimous vote; *passed me* approved by me   72 *Traduced* slandered   73 *faculties* qualities

The chronicles of my doing, let me say
75 'Tis but the fate of place and the rough brake
76 That virtue must go through. We must not stint
Our necessary actions in the fear
78 To cope malicious censurers, which ever,
As rav'nous fishes, do a vessel follow
80 That is new-trimmed, but benefit no further
Than vainly longing. What we oft do best,
82 By sick interpreters (once weak ones) is
83 Not ours, or not allowed; what worst, as oft
84 Hitting a grosser quality, is cried up
For our best act. If we shall stand still,
86 In fear our motion will be mocked or carped at,
We should take root here where we sit,
88 Or sit state-statues only.
KING   Things done well
And with a care exempt themselves from fear;
90 Things done without example, in their issue
Are to be feared. Have you a precedent
Of this commission? I believe, not any.
93 We must not rend our subjects from our laws
94 And stick them in our will. Sixth part of each?
95 A trembling contribution! Why, we take
96 From every tree lop, bark, and part o' th' timber;
And though we leave it with a root, thus hacked,
The air will drink the sap. To every county
Where this is questioned, send our letters with
100 Free pardon to each man that has denied
101 The force of this commission. Pray look to't.

---

75 *place* high office; *brake* thicket   76 *stint* cease to do   78 *cope* encounter
80 *new-trimmed* newly fitted   82 *sick* envious, malicious   83 *Not ours* not
credited to us; *allowed* approved   84 *Hitting . . . quality* appealing to the (ignorant) masses   86 *motion* (1) movement, (2) proposal   88 *state-statues* i.e.,
mere statues of statesmen   90 *example* legitimizing precedent; *issue* outcome
93 *rend* tear (away)   94 *stick . . . will* i.e., make them subject only to our
capricious will   95 *trembling* fearful   96 *lop* the crown of the tree   101
force lawful authority

I put it to your care.
WOLSEY   *[Aside to the Secretary]*
                      A word with you.
Let there be letters writ to every shire
Of the king's grace and pardon. The grievèd commons   104
Hardly conceive of me. Let it be noised   105
That through our intercession this revokement
And pardon comes. I shall anon advise you
Further in the proceeding.   ·   *Exit Secretary.*
    Enter Surveyor.
KATHERINE
I am sorry that the Duke of Buckingham
Is run in your displeasure.   110
KING   It grieves many.
The gentleman is learned and a most rare speaker,
To nature none more bound; his training such   112
That he may furnish and instruct great teachers
And never seek for aid out of himself. Yet see,   114
When these so noble benefits shall prove
Not well disposed, the mind growing once corrupt,   116
They turn to vicious forms, ten times more ugly   117
Than ever they were fair. This man so complete,   118
Who was enrolled 'mongst wonders – and when we,   ·
Almost with ravished list'ning, could not find   *120*
His hour of speech a minute – he, my lady,
Hath into monstrous habits put the graces   122
That once were his, and is become as black
As if besmeared in hell. Sit by us. You shall hear
(This was his gentleman in trust) of him
Things to strike honor sad. Bid him recount
The fore-recited practices, whereof   127
We cannot feel too little, hear too much.

---

104 *grace* mercy   **105** *Hardly conceive* think harshly; *noised* rumored   **110** *Is run in* has incurred   **112** *bound* indebted   **114** *out of* outside of   **116** *disposed* directed   **117** *vicious* evil   **118** *complete* accomplished   **122** *habits* costumes (i.e., guises)   **127** *practices* intrigues

WOLSEY
    Stand forth, and with bold spirit relate what you
130   Most like a careful subject have collected
    Out of the Duke of Buckingham.
KING   Speak freely.
SURVEYOR
    First, it was usual with him – every day
    It would infect his speech – that if the king
134   Should without issue die, he'll carry it so
    To make the scepter his. These very words
    I've heard him utter to his son-in-law,
    Lord Aberga'ny, to whom by oath he menaced
    Revenge upon the cardinal.
WOLSEY   .   Please your highness note
    This dangerous conception in this point:
140   Not friended by his wish to your high person,
    His will is most malignant, and it stretches
    Beyond you to your friends.
KATHERINE   My learned lord cardinal,
143   Deliver all with charity.
KING   Speak on.
    How grounded he his title to the crown   .
145   Upon our fail? To this point hast thou heard him
    At any time speak aught?
SURVEYOR   He was brought to this
147   By a vain prophecy of Nicholas Henton.
KING
    What was that Henton?
SURVEYOR   Sir, a Chartreux friar,
    His confessor, who fed him every minute
150   With words of sovereignty.
KING   How know'st thou this?

130–31 collected/Out of gathered from or about   134 issue progeny; carry it
so contrive   140 friended by gratified in (i.e., the wish that the king will die
without an heir)   143 Deliver relate   145 fail (1) death, (2) failure to produce an heir   147 Henton (otherwise Michael Hopkins; see I.1.221)

SURVEYOR
Not long before your highness sped to France,
The duke being at the Rose, within the parish   152
Saint Lawrence Poultney, did of me demand
What was the speech among the Londoners
Concerning the French journey. I replied,
Men feared the French would prove perfidious,
To the king's danger. Presently the duke   157
Said 'twas the fear indeed, and that he doubted   158
'Twould prove the verity of certain words
Spoke by a holy monk "that oft," says he,   160
"Hath sent to me, wishing me to permit
John de la Car, my chaplain, a choice hour
To hear from him a matter of some moment;
Whom after under the confession's seal
He solemnly had sworn that what he spoke
My chaplain to no creature living but
To me should utter, with demure confidence   167
This pausingly ensued: neither the king nor's heirs   168
(Tell you the duke) shall prosper. Bid him strive
To [win] the love o' th' commonalty. The duke   170
Shall govern England."
KATHERINE   If I know you well,
You were the duke's surveyor and lost your office
On the complaint o' th' tenants. Take good heed
You charge not in your spleen a noble person   174
And spoil your nobler soul. I say, take heed;   175
Yes, heartily beseech you.
KING   Let him on.
Go forward.
SURVEYOR   On my soul, I'll speak but truth.
I told my lord the duke, by th' devil's illusions   178

---

152 *Rose* i.e., Manor of the Red Rose, belonging to Buckingham 157
Presently immediately 158 *doubted* feared 167 *demure confidence* solemn
conviction 168 *pausingly* with pauses between words 170 *commonalty*
common people 174 *spleen* malice 175 *spoil* ruin 178 *illusions* decep-
tions

The monk might be deceived; and that 'twas dangerous
180 To ruminate on this so far until
181 It forged him some design, which, being believed,
182 It was much like to do. He answered, "Tush,
It can do me no damage!" adding further
184 That, had the king in his last sickness failed,
The cardinal's and Sir Thomas Lovell's heads
186 Should have gone off.
KING   Ha! What, so rank? Ah, ha!
There's mischief in this man. Canst thou say further?
SURVEYOR
I can, my liege.
KING   Proceed.
SURVEYOR   Being at Greenwich,
After your highness had reproved the duke
190 About Sir William Bulmer –
KING   I remember
Of such a time. Being my sworn servant,
The duke retained him his. But on: what hence?
SURVEYOR
"If," quoth he, "I for this had been committed,
As to the Tower I thought, I would have played
The part my father meant to act upon
196 Th' usurper Richard, who, being at Salisbury,
Made suit to come in's presence, which if granted,
198 As he made semblance of his duty, would
Have put his knife into him."
KING   A giant traitor!
WOLSEY
200 Now, madam, may his highness live in freedom,
And this man out of prison?
KATHERINE   God mend all.

---

181 *forged* shaped   **182** *to do* i.e., to bring him into danger   **184** *failed* died
186 *rank* (1) grossly corrupt, (2) rebellious   **196** *Th' usurper Richard* i.e.,
Richard III (cf. Shakespeare's play so titled)   **198** *made semblance . . . duty*
feigned homage

KING
    There's something more would out of thee. What say'st?
SURVEYOR
    After "the duke his father," with the "knife,"
    He stretched him, and, with one hand on his dagger,   204
    Another spread on's breast, mounting his eyes,   205
    He did discharge a horrible oath, whose tenor
    Was, were he evil used, he would outgo   207
    His father by as much as a performance
    Does an irresolute purpose.   209
KING   There's his period,
    To sheathe his knife in us. He is attached;   210
    Call him to present trial. If he may   211
    Find mercy in the law, 'tis his: if none,
    Let him not seek't of us. By day and night,
    He's traitor to th' height!   _Exeunt._   214

                              *

∾ **I.3** *Enter Lord Chamberlain and Lord Sandys.*

CHAMBERLAIN
    Is't possible the spells of France should juggle   1
    Men into such strange mysteries?   2
SANDYS   New customs,
    Though they be never so ridiculous
    (Nay, let 'em be unmanly), yet are followed.
CHAMBERLAIN
    As far as I see, all the good our English
    Have got by the late voyage is but merely
    A fit or two o' th' face; but they are shrewd ones,   7
    For when they hold 'em, you would swear directly   8

---

204 *stretched him* drew himself up   205 *mounting* raising   207 *evil used*
mistreated   209 *period* goal, conclusion   210 *attached* arrested   211 *present* immediate   214 *to th' height* in the highest degree
    I.3 The royal palace   1 *juggle* trick   2 *strange mysteries* i.e., bizarre fashions
7 *A fit . . . face* i.e., odd grimaces   8 *hold 'em* i.e., keep their expressions fixed

Their very noses had been counselors
10   To Pepin or Clotharius, they keep state so.
SANDYS
11   They have all new legs, and lame ones. One would take
     it,
12   That never see 'em pace before, the spavin,
13   A springhalt reigned among 'em.
CHAMBERLAIN   Death my lord,
14   Their clothes are after such a pagan cut to't
     That sure th' have worn out Christendom.
         Enter Sir Thomas Lovell.   How now?
     What news, Sir Thomas Lovell?
LOVELL   Faith, my lord,
     I hear of none but the new proclamation
     That's clapped upon the court gate.
CHAMBERLAIN   What is't for?
LOVELL
     The reformation of our traveled gallants
20   That fill the court with quarrels, talk, and tailors.
CHAMBERLAIN
     I'm glad 'tis there. Now I would pray our monsieurs
     To think an English courtier may be wise
     And never see the Louvre.
LOVELL   They must either
     (For so run the conditions) leave those remnants
25   Of fool and feather that they got in France,
26   With all their honorable points of ignorance
27   Pertaining thereunto – as fights and fireworks;
     Abusing better men than they can be,

---

10 *Pepin, Clotharius* early kings of France; *keep state* maintain their loftiness
11 *legs* ways of walking and/or bowing (making a leg)   **12** *pace* strut; *spavin*
tumor on the leg of a horse   **13** *springhalt* crippling ailment of a horse's
sinews   **14** *to't* furthermore   **25** *fool and feather* (folly and extravagant feath-
ers are connected here)   **26** *honorable . . . ignorance* points they ignorantly
regard as ones of honor   **27** *fights and fireworks* mock battles and fireworks
displays (*fireworks* possibly alluding to whoring as well)

Out of a foreign wisdom – renouncing clean   29
The faith they have in tennis and tall stockings,   30
Short blistered breeches, and those types of travel,   31
And understand again like honest men,
Or pack to their old playfellows. There, I take it,   33
They may *cum privilegio* "wee" away   34
The lag end of their lewdness and be laughed at.   35
SANDYS
'Tis time to give 'em physic, their diseases
Are grown so catching.
CHAMBERLAIN   What a loss our ladies
Will have of these trim vanities!   38
LOVELL   Ay, marry,
There will be woe indeed, lords. The sly whoresons   39
Have got a speeding trick to lay down ladies.   40
A French song and a fiddle has no fellow.
SANDYS
The devil fiddle 'em! I am glad they are going,
For sure there's no converting of 'em. Now
An honest country lord, as I am, beaten
A long time out of play, may bring his plain song   45
And have an hour of hearing, and, by'r Lady,   46
Held current music too.   47
CHAMBERLAIN   Well said, Lord Sandys.
Your colt's tooth is not cast yet?   48
SANDYS   No, my lord,
Nor shall not while I have a stump.   49
CHAMBERLAIN   Sir Thomas,

---

29 *Out of* on the strength of   31 *blistered* puffed-out; *types* tokens   33 *pack*
be sent packing   34 *cum privilegio* with immunity; *wee* (Englishman's comic
pronunciation of *oui*)   35 *lag end* remainder; *lewdness* (1) ignorance, (2) las-
civiousness   38 *trim vanities* stylish trifles   39 *whoresons* bastards (collo-
quial)   40 *speeding* effective   45 *play* i.e., sexual action; *plain song* simple
tune, alluding to the unadorned melodies of the medieval church   46 *by'r
Lady* (oath on the name of the Virgin Mary)   47 *current* acceptable, good (as
currency)   48 *colt's tooth* (proverbial for youthful wantonness); *cast* fallen out
49 *stump* i.e., of a tooth, but implying penis

50   Whither were you agoing?
LOVELL   To the cardinal's.
      Your lordship is a guest too.
CHAMBERLAIN   O, 'tis true;
52   This night he makes a supper, and a great one,
      To many lords and ladies. There will be
      The beauty of this kingdom, I'll assure you.
LOVELL
      That churchman bears a bounteous mind indeed,
      A hand as fruitful as the land that feeds us;
      His dews fall everywhere.
CHAMBERLAIN   No doubt he's noble.
58   He had a black mouth that said other of him.
SANDYS
59   He may, my lord; has wherewithal. In him
60   Sparing would show a worse sin than ill doctrine.
61   Men of his way should be most liberal;
      They are set here for examples.
CHAMBERLAIN   True, they are so;
      But few now give so great ones. My barge stays;
      Your lordship shall along. Come, good Sir Thomas,
      We shall be late else; which I would not be,
66   For I was spoke to, with Sir Henry Guilford
67   This night to be comptrollers.
SANDYS   I am your lordship's.
                                          Exeunt.

                        *

---

52 *makes* gives   58 *black* evil, malignant   59 *He may* he is able to   61 *way*
way of life, calling; *liberal* generous   66 *spoke to* asked   67 *comptrollers* stew-
ards

& **I.4** *Hautboys. A small table under a state for the Cardinal, a longer table for the guests. Then enter Anne Bullen and divers other Ladies and Gentlemen, as guests at one door; at another door enter Sir Henry Guilford.*

GUILFORD
Ladies, a general welcome from his grace
Salutes ye all. This night he dedicates
To fair content and you. None here, he hopes,
In all this noble bevy, has brought with her   4
One care abroad. He would have all as merry
As first, good company, good wine, good welcome   6
Can make good people.
      Enter Lord Chamberlain, Lord Sandys, and Lovell.
                              O my lord, you're tardy!
The very thought of this fair company
Clapped wings to me.
CHAMBERLAIN   You are young, Sir Harry Guilford.
SANDYS
Sir Thomas Lovell, had the cardinal   10
But half my lay thoughts in him, some of these   11
Should find a running banquet ere they rested,   12
I think would better please 'em. By my life,
They are a sweet society of fair ones.
LOVELL
O that your lordship were but now confessor
To one or two of these!
SANDYS   ·   I would I were.
They should find easy penance.
LOVELL   Faith, how easy?

I.4 York Place **s.d.** *Hautboys* oboelike instruments (play); *state* chair of state
4 *bevy* company (ladies emphasized)   **6** *As first* i.e., first . . . then . . . then
11 *lay* secular   **12** *running* speedy (sexually eyeing the ladies; the joke continues through l. 18, with additional innuendo of spanking)

SANDYS
    As easy as a down bed would afford it.
CHAMBERLAIN
    Sweet ladies, will it please you sit? Sir Harry,
20 Place you that side; I'll take the charge of this.
    His grace is ent'ring. Nay, you must not freeze!
    Two women placed together makes cold weather.
    My Lord Sandys, you are one will keep 'em waking.
    Pray sit between these ladies.
SANDYS   By my faith,
    And thank your lordship. By your leave, sweet ladies,
        [Seats himself between Anne Bullen and another lady.]
    If I chance to talk a little wild, forgive me;
    I had it from my father.
ANNE   Was he mad, sir?
SANDYS
    O very mad, exceeding mad, in love too.
    But he would bite none. Just as I do now,
30 He would kiss you twenty with a breath.
        [Kisses her.]
CHAMBERLAIN   Well said, my lord.
31 So now you're fairly seated. Gentlemen,
    The penance lies on you if these fair ladies
33 Pass away frowning.
SANDYS   For my little cure,
34 Let me alone.
        Hautboys. Enter Cardinal Wolsey, [attended,] and
        takes his state.
WOLSEY
    You're welcome, my fair guests. That noble lady
    Or gentleman that is not freely merry
    Is not my friend. This to confirm my welcome;
    And to you all, good health.

---

20 *Place you* you assign seats   **30** *kiss you* kiss; *Well said* well done   **31** *fairly*
properly   **33** *cure* clerical responsibility (to his "parishioners")   **34** *Let me*
alone i.e., I can handle it; **s.d.** *state* chair of state

[Drinks.]

SANDYS   Your grace is noble.
  Let me have such a bowl may hold my thanks
  And save me so much talking.   40
WOLSEY   My Lord Sandys,
  I am beholding to you: cheer your neighbors.   41
  Ladies, you are not merry; gentlemen,
  Whose fault is this?
SANDYS   The red wine first must rise
  In their fair cheeks, my lord; then we shall have 'em
  Talk us to silence.   45
ANNE   You are a merry gamester,
  My Lord Sandys.   46
SANDYS   Yes, if I make my play.
  Here's to your ladyship, and pledge it, madam,
  For 'tis to such a thing –
ANNE   You cannot show me.
SANDYS
  I told your grace they would talk anon.   49
       Drum and trumpet. Chambers discharged.
WOLSEY   What's that?
CHAMBERLAIN
  Look out there, some of ye.   *[Exit a Servant.]* 50
WOLSEY   What warlike voice,
  And to what end is this? Nay ladies, fear not.
  By all the laws of war you're privileged.   52
       Enter a Servant.
CHAMBERLAIN
  How now, what is't?
SERVANT   A noble troop of strangers
  For so they seem. Th' have left their barge and landed,
  And hither make, as great ambassadors

---

41 *beholding* obliged   45 *gamester* joker, player of sexual games   46 *make
my play* (1) win, (2) plead my cause   49 s.d. *Chambers* small cannons (which
probably set fire to the Globe theater in 1613; see Introduction); *discharged*
fired   52 *you're privileged* you have immunity

From foreign princes.
WOLSEY   Good lord chamberlain,
Go, give 'em welcome; you can speak the French
tongue.
And pray receive 'em nobly and conduct 'em
Into our presence, where this heaven of beauty
60   Shall shine at full upon them. Some attend him!
                    [*Exit Chamberlain, attended.*]
         All rise, and tables removed.
61   You have now a broken banquet, but we'll mend it.
A good digestion to you all, and once more
63   I show'r a welcome on ye: welcome all.
         Hautboys. Enter King and others, as masquers,
         habited like shepherds, ushered by the Lord
         Chamberlain. They pass directly before the Cardinal
         and gracefully salute him.
A noble company! What are their pleasures?
CHAMBERLAIN
Because they speak no English, thus they prayed
66   To tell your grace: that having heard by fame
Of this so noble and so fair assembly
This night to meet here, they could do no less
(Out of the great respect they bear to beauty)
70   But leave their flocks and, under your fair conduct,
Crave leave to view these ladies and entreat
An hour of revels with 'em.
WOLSEY   Say, lord chamberlain,
They have done my poor house grace; for which I pay
'em
74   A thousand thanks and pray 'em take their pleasures.
         Choose ladies. King and Anne Bullen.
KING
The fairest hand I ever touched: O beauty,

---

61 *broken* interrupted 63 s.d. *masquers* masked dancers or performers;
habited dressed 66 *fame* report 70 *conduct* guidance 74 s.d. *Choose . . .*
Bullen the men choose partners; Henry chooses Anne Bullen

Till now I never knew thee!
Music. Dance.
WOLSEY
My lord!
CHAMBERLAIN   Your grace?
WOLSEY   Pray tell 'em thus much from
    me:
There should be one amongst 'em, by his person,
More worthy this place than myself; to whom,   79
If I but knew him, with my love and duty   80
I would surrender it.
CHAMBERLAIN   I will, my lord.
    Whisper [with the Masquers].
WOLSEY
What say they?
CHAMBERLAIN   Such a one they all confess
There is indeed, which they would have your grace
Find out, and he will take it.   84
WOLSEY   Let me see then –
By all your good leaves, gentlemen; here I'll make
My royal choice.
KING   *[Unmasks.]* Ye have found him, cardinal.
You hold a fair assembly. You do well, lord.
You are a churchman, or I'll tell you, cardinal,
I should judge now unhappily.   89
WOLSEY   I am glad
Your grace is grown so pleasant.   90
KING   My lord chamberlain,
Prithee come hither. What fair lady's that?
CHAMBERLAIN
An't please your grace, Sir Thomas Bullen's daughter,
The Viscount Rochford, one of her highness' women.

---

79 *place* position of eminence   84 *Find out* identify; *it* i.e., the place of
honor   89 *unhappily* unfavorably (of his princely display)   90 *pleasant* humorous

KING
　　By heaven she is a dainty one. Sweetheart,
95　　I were unmannerly to take you out
　　And not to kiss you. *[Kisses her.]* A health, gentlemen!
97　　Let it go round.
WOLSEY
　　Sir Thomas Lovell, is the banquet ready
　　I' th' privy chamber?
LOVELL　　　　　　　　　　Yes, my lord.
WOLSEY　　　　　　　　　　　　　Your grace,
100　　I fear, with dancing is a little heated.
KING
　　I fear, too much.
WOLSEY　　　　　　There's fresher air, my lord,
　　In the next chamber.
KING
　　Lead in your ladies ev'ry one. Sweet partner,
　　I must not yet forsake you. Let's be merry,
　　Good my lord cardinal. I have half a dozen healths
106　　To drink to these fair ladies, and a measure
　　To lead 'em once again; and then let's dream
108　　Who's best in favor. Let the music knock it.
　　　　　　　　　　　　　　　　Exeunt with Trumpets.

*

❧ **II.1** *Enter two Gentlemen at several doors.*

FIRST GENTLEMAN
　　Whither away so fast?
SECOND GENTLEMAN　　O, God save ye!
2　　Ev'n to the Hall, to hear what shall become
　　Of the great Duke of Buckingham.

---

95 *take you out* lead you out to the dance　97 *it* i.e., the cup　100 *heated* (implying sexually aroused)　106 *measure* dance　108 *in favor* i.e., (1) with the ladies, (2) in looks; *knock it* strike up; **s.d.** *Trumpets* trumpeters
　II.1 A street s.d. *several* separate　2 *the Hall* Westminster Hall

FIRST GENTLEMAN   I'll save you
That labor, sir. All's now done but the ceremony
Of bringing back the prisoner.
SECOND GENTLEMAN   Were you there?
FIRST GENTLEMAN
Yes indeed was I.
SECOND GENTLEMAN
                    Pray speak what has happened.
FIRST GENTLEMAN
You may guess quickly what.
SECOND GENTLEMAN   Is he found guilty?
FIRST GENTLEMAN
Yes truly is he, and condemned upon't.
SECOND GENTLEMAN
I am sorry for't.
FIRST GENTLEMAN
                    So are a number more.
SECOND GENTLEMAN
But pray how passed it?   10
FIRST GENTLEMAN
I'll tell you in a little. The great duke   11
Came to the bar; where to his accusations
He pleaded still not guilty, and alleged   13
Many sharp reasons to defeat the law.   14
The king's attorney, on the contrary,   15
Urged on the examinations, proofs, confessions   16
Of divers witnesses, which the duke desired
To him brought *viva voce* to his face;   18
At which appeared against him his surveyor,
Sir Gilbert Perk his chancellor, and John Car,   20
Confessor to him, with that devil monk,
Hopkins, that made this mischief.

---

10 *passed it* did the trial proceed   11 *in a little* briefly   13 *alleged* put forward   14 *sharp reasons* acute arguments   15 *on the contrary* opposing these
arguments   16 *Urged on* pressed as evidence   18 *viva voce* in person (literally, "with living voice")   20 *chancellor* secretary

SECOND GENTLEMAN   That was he
  That fed him with his prophecies.
FIRST GENTLEMAN   The same.
24 All these accused him strongly, which he fain
    Would have flung from him, but indeed he could not;
    And so his peers upon this evidence
    Have found him guilty of high treason. Much
    He spoke, and learnedly for life; but all
    Was either pitied in him or forgotten.
SECOND GENTLEMAN
30 After all this how did he bear himself?
FIRST GENTLEMAN
    When he was brought again to th' bar, to hear
32 His knell rung out, his judgment, he was stirred
    With such an agony he sweat extremely
34 And something spoke in choler, ill and hasty;
35 But he fell to himself again, and sweetly
    In all the rest showed a most noble patience.
SECOND GENTLEMAN
    I do not think he fears death.
FIRST GENTLEMAN   Sure he does not;
    He never was so womanish. The cause
    He may a little grieve at.
SECOND GENTLEMAN   Certainly
40 The cardinal is the end of this.
FIRST GENTLEMAN   'Tis likely
41 By all conjectures: first Kildare's attendure,
42 Then Deputy of Ireland, who removed,
    Earl Surrey was sent thither, and in haste too,
44 Lest he should help his father.
SECOND GENTLEMAN   That trick of state
45 Was a deep envious one.

---

24 *fain* wishfully   32 *knell* passing bell; *judgment* sentence   34 *choler* anger
35 *fell to himself* regained self-control   40 *end* cause   41 *attendure* attainder
(confiscation of the earl's estate, upon the death sentence)   42 *Deputy*
viceroy (governor)   44 *father* i.e., father-in-law (Surrey was Buckingham's
son-in-law)   45 *envious* malicious (on Wolsey's part)

FIRST GENTLEMAN   At his return
No doubt he will requite it. This is noted   46
(And generally): whoever the king favors,   47
The card'nal instantly will find employment,
And far enough from court too.
SECOND GENTLEMAN   All the commons
Hate him perniciously, and o' my conscience   50
Wish him ten fathom deep. This duke as much
They love and dote on, call him bounteous Bucking-
ham
The mirror of all courtesy –   53
    Enter Buckingham from his arraignment; Tipstaves
    before him; [Officer bearing] the [executioner's] ax
    with the edge towards him; Halberds on each side;
    accompanied with Sir Thomas Lovell, Sir Nicholas
    Vaux, Sir Walter Sandys, and common people, etc.
FIRST GENTLEMAN   Stay there, sir,
And see the noble ruined man you speak of.
SECOND GENTLEMAN
Let's stand close and behold him.
BUCKINGHAM   All good people,
You that thus far have come to pity me,
Hear what I say and then go home and lose me.   57
I have this day received a traitor's judgment   58
And by that name must die. Yet heaven bear witness,
And if I have a conscience, let it sink me   60
Even as the ax falls, if I be not faithful!   61
The law I bear no malice for my death,
'T has done upon the premises but justice;   63
But those that sought it I could wish more Christians.
Be what they will, I heartily forgive 'em.

---

46 *requite it* pay it back   47 *generally* by everyone   50 *perniciously* to the
death   53 *mirror* model; *courtesy* courtly conduct; **s.d.** *Tipstaves* officers who
took the accused from court into custody (so called because they carried
staves tipped with silver); *Halberds* halberdiers (carrying long-handled battle-
axes with spear points)   57 *lose* forget   58 *judgment* sentence   60 *sink* de-
stroy, condemn   61 *faithful* loyal   63 *upon the premises* given the evidence

66 Yet let 'em look they glory not in mischief,
67 Nor build their evils on the graves of great men;
   For then my guiltless blood must cry against 'em.
   For further life in this world I ne'er hope,
70 Nor will I sue, although the king have mercies
71 More than I dare make faults. You few that loved me
   And dare be bold to weep for Buckingham,
   His noble friends and fellows, whom to leave
74 Is only bitter to him, only dying,
   Go with me like good angels to my end;
   And, as the long divorce of steel falls on me,
77 Make of your prayers one sweet sacrifice
78 And lift my soul to heaven. Lead on a God's name.

LOVELL
   I do beseech your grace, for charity,
80 If ever any malice in your heart
   Were hid against me, now to forgive me frankly.

BUCKINGHAM
   Sir Thomas Lovell, I as free forgive you
   As I would be forgiven. I forgive all.
   There cannot be those numberless offenses
85 'Gainst me that I cannot take peace with. No black
     envy
   Shall mark my grave. Commend me to his grace;
   And if he speak of Buckingham, pray tell him
   You met him half in heaven. My vows and prayers
89 Yet are the king's, and till my soul forsake
90 Shall cry for blessings on him. May he live
91 Longer than I have time to tell his years;
   Ever beloved and loving may his rule be;
93 And when old time shall lead him to his end,
94 Goodness and he fill up one monument!

---

66 *look* take care   67 *build . . . graves of* erect their evil designs on the death
of   71 *make faults* commit offenses   74 *Is only . . . dying* is the only thing
bitter to him, the only death   77 *sacrifice* offering   78 *a* in   85 *envy* malice
89 *forsake* leave the body   91 *tell* count   93 *old time* old age   94 *monument*
tomb

LOVELL
> To th' waterside I must conduct your grace,
> Then give my charge up to Sir Nicholas Vaux,
> Who undertakes you to your end.   97
VAUX   Prepare there,
> The duke is coming. See the barge be ready
> And fit it with such furniture as suits   99
> The greatness of his person.   100
BUCKINGHAM   Nay, Sir Nicholas,
> Let it alone; my state now will but mock me.   101
> When I came hither I was Lord High Constable
> And Duke of Buckingham; now poor Edward Bohun.
> Yet I am richer than my base accusers,
> That never knew what truth meant. I now seal it,   105
> And with that blood will make 'em one day groan for't.
> My noble father, Henry of Buckingham,
> Who first raised head against usurping Richard,   108
> Flying for succor to his servant Banister,
> Being distressed, was by that wretch betrayed,   110
> And without trial fell. God's peace be with him!
> Henry the Seventh succeeding, truly pitying
> My father's loss, like a most royal prince
> Restored me to my honors; and out of ruins
> Made my name once more noble. Now his son,
> Henry the Eighth, life, honor, name, and all
> That made me happy, at one stroke has taken
> For ever from the world. I had my trial,
> And must needs say a noble one; which makes me
> A little happier than my wretched father.   120
> Yet thus far we are one in fortunes: both
> Fell by our servants, by those men we loved most —
> A most unnatural and faithless service.
> Heaven has an end in all; yet you that hear me,   124

---

97 *undertakes* conducts   99 *furniture* equipment   101 *state* noble accoutrements   105 *seal* ratify   108 *raised head* gathered a force   124 *end* purpose

125 This from a dying man receive as certain:
Where you are liberal of your loves and counsels
127 Be sure you be not loose; for those you make friends
And give your hearts to, when they once perceive
129 The least rub in your fortunes, fall away
130 Like water from ye, never found again
131 But where they mean to sink ye. All good people,
Pray for me! I must now forsake ye; the last hour
Of my long weary life is come upon me.
Farewell!
And when you would say something that is sad,
Speak how I fell. I have done, and God forgive me!
                                    Exeunt Duke and train.

FIRST GENTLEMAN
137 O this is full of pity! Sir, it calls,
I fear, too many curses on their heads
That were the authors.

SECOND GENTLEMAN   If the duke be guiltless,
140 'Tis full of woe. Yet I can give you inkling
141 Of an ensuing evil, if it fall,
Greater than this.

FIRST GENTLEMAN   Good angels keep it from us!
143 What may it be? You do not doubt my faith, sir?

SECOND GENTLEMAN
This secret is so weighty 'twill require
A strong faith to conceal it.

FIRST GENTLEMAN   Let me have it.
146 I do not talk much.

SECOND GENTLEMAN I am confident.
You shall, sir. Did you not of late days hear
148 A buzzing of a separation
149 Between the king and Katherine?

FIRST GENTLEMAN   Yes, but it held not;

---

125 *receive as certain* accept as truth 127 *loose* unrestrained 129 *rub* obstruction 131 *sink* ruin 137 *calls* calls down 141 *fall* occur 143 *faith* trustworthiness 146 *I am confident* I trust you 148 *buzzing* rumor 149 *held not* did not continue

    For when the king once heard it, out of anger   *150*
    He sent command to the lord mayor straight   151
    To stop the rumor and allay those tongues   152
    That durst disperse it.
SECOND GENTLEMAN   But that slander, sir,
    Is found a truth now; for it grows again
    Fresher than e'er it was, and held for certain   155
    The king will venture at it. Either the cardinal,
    Or some about him near, have out of malice
    To the good queen possessed him with a scruple   158
    That will undo her. To confirm this too,
    Cardinal Campeius is arrived, and lately,   160
    As all think, for this business.
FIRST GENTLEMAN   'Tis the cardinal;
    And merely to revenge him on the emperor   162
    For not bestowing on him at his asking
    The archbishopric of Toledo, this is purposed.   164
SECOND GENTLEMAN
    I think you have hit the mark. But is't not cruel
    That she should feel the smart of this? The cardinal   166
    Will have his will, and she must fall.
FIRST GENTLEMAN   'Tis woeful.
    We are too open here to argue this;   168
    Let's think in private more.   *Exeunt.*

*

∾ **II.2** *Enter Lord Chamberlain, reading this letter.*

[CHAMBERLAIN]   "My lord, the horses your lordship sent
    for, with all the care I had, I saw well chosen, ridden, 2
    and furnished. They were young and handsome and of 3

---

151 *straight* straightaway   152 *allay* restrain   155 *held* accepted   158 *possessed . . . scruple* raised a doubt in his mind   162 *the emperor* Charles V (Holy Roman Emperor and nephew of Queen Katherine)   164 *purposed* intended   166 *smart* sting   168 *open* exposed in public
    II.2 The royal palace   2 *ridden* broken in   3 *furnished* equipped

the best breed in the north. When they were ready to
set out for London, a man of my lord cardinal's by
6   commission and main power took 'em from me, with
this reason: his master would be served before a subject,
if not before the king; which stopped our mouths, sir."
I fear he will indeed. Well, let him have them.
10   He will have all, I think.
>*Enter to the Lord Chamberlain the Dukes of Norfolk*
>*and Suffolk.*

NORFOLK
Well met, my lord chamberlain.
CHAMBERLAIN
Good day to both your graces.
SUFFOLK
How is the king employed?
CHAMBERLAIN   I left him private,
14   Full of sad thoughts and troubles.
NORFOLK   What's the cause?
CHAMBERLAIN
It seems the marriage with his brother's wife
Has crept too near his conscience.
SUFFOLK *[Aside]*   No, his conscience
Has crept too near another lady.
NORFOLK   'Tis so.
This is the cardinal's doing. The king-cardinal,
19   That blind priest, like the eldest son of Fortune,
20   Turns what he list. The king will know him one day.
SUFFOLK
Pray God he do; he'll never know himself else.
NORFOLK
How holily he works in all his business
23   And with what zeal! For, now he has cracked the league
Between us and the emperor, the queen's great nephew,
He dives into the king's soul, and there scatters

---
6 *commission* legal writ; *main power* brute force   14 *sad* serious 19 *blind*
i.e., arbitrary 23 *cracked* broken

Dangers, doubts, wringing of the conscience,   26
Fears, and despairs, and all these for his marriage.
And out of all these, to restore the king,
He counsels a divorce, a loss of her
That like a jewel has hung twenty years   30
About his neck, yet never lost her luster;
Of her that loves him with that excellence   32
That angels love good men with; even of her
That, when the greatest stroke of fortune falls,   34
Will bless the king. And is not this course pious?
CHAMBERLAIN
Heaven keep me from such counsel! 'Tis most true
These news are everywhere, every tongue speaks 'em,
And every true heart weeps for't. All that dare
Look into these affairs see this main end: 39
The French king's sister. Heaven will one day open   40
The king's eyes that so long have slept upon   41
This bold bad man.
SUFFOLK   And free us from his slavery.
NORFOLK
We had need pray,   43
And heartily, for our deliverance,   44
Or this imperious man will work us all
From princes into pages. All men's honors
Lie like one lump before him, to be fashioned   47
Into what pitch he please.   48
SUFFOLK   For me, my lords,
I love him not, nor fear him. There's my creed:
As I am made without him, so I'll stand,   50
If the king please. His curses and his blessings
Touch me alike; th' are breath I not believe in.
I knew him, and I know him: so I leave him

---

26 *wringing* torture   30 *jewel* gold chain (worn by men)   32 *excellence* virtuous devotion   34 *stroke* blow   39 *end* object   41 *slept upon* been closed to
43 *had need* had better   44 *heartily* wholeheartedly   47 *lump* i.e., lump of
clay   48 *pitch* level, status   50 *stand* stand firm, remain

To him that made him proud, the pope.

NORFOLK   Let's in,
And with some other business put the king
From these sad thoughts that work too much upon
   him.
My lord, you'll bear us company?

CHAMBERLAIN   Excuse me.
The king has sent me otherwhere. Besides,
You'll find a most unfit time to disturb him.

60   Health to your lordships!

NORFOLK   Thanks, my good lord chamberlain.   *Exit Lord Chamberlain; and the King draws
                  the curtain and sits reading pensively.*

SUFFOLK
61   How sad he looks. Sure he is much afflicted.

KING
Who's there, ha?

NORFOLK   Pray God he be not angry.

KING
Who's there, I say? How dare you thrust yourselves
Into my private meditations?
Who am I? ha?

NORFOLK
A gracious king that pardons all offenses
67   Malice ne'er meant. Our breach of duty this way
68   Is business of estate; in which we come
To know your royal pleasure.

KING   Ye are too bold.
70   Go to! I'll make ye know your times of business.
71   Is this an hour for temporal affairs? ha?
         Enter Wolsey and Campeius with a commission.
Who's there? My good lord cardinal? O my Wolsey,
The quiet of my wounded conscience;

---

61 *sad* serious; *afflicted* troubled   67 *Malice* evil intent; *this way* in this respect   68 *estate* state   71 *temporal* worldly

Thou art a cure fit for a king. *[To Campeius]* You're wel-
come,
Most learned reverend sir, into our kingdom.
Use us and it. *[To Wolsey]* My good lord, have great care
I be not found a talker.   77
WOLSEY   Sir, you cannot.
I would your grace would give us but an hour
Of private conference.
KING   *[To Norfolk and Suffolk]*
                          We are busy: go.
NORFOLK   *[Aside to Suffolk]*
This priest has no pride in him?   80
SUFFOLK   *[Aside to Norfolk]*   Not to speak of.
I would not be so sick though for his place.   81
But this cannot continue.
NORFOLK   *[Aside to Suffolk]* If it do,
I'll venture one; have at him!   83
SUFFOLK   *[Aside to Norfolk]*   I another.
                          Exeunt Norfolk and Suffolk.
WOLSEY
Your grace has given a precedent of wisdom
Above all princes in committing freely
Your scruple to the voice of Christendom.   86
Who can be angry now? What envy reach you?   87
The Spaniard, tied by blood and favor to her,
Must now confess, if they have any goodness,
The trial just and noble. All the clerks   90
(I mean the learned ones in Christian kingdoms)
Have their free voices. Rome, the nurse of judgment,   92
Invited by your noble self, hath sent
One general tongue unto us, this good man,   94
This just and learned priest, Cardinal Campeius,

---

77 *I . . . talker* i.e., that this not turn out to be idle talk   81 *sick . . . place*
i.e., sick with pride even to gain his position   83 *I'll . . . one* i.e., I'll be one
of those who take him on; *have at him* (a challenge, directed aside at Wolsey)
86 *voice* vote   87 *envy* malice   90 *clerks* scholars   92 *voices* votes   94 *general tongue* spokesperson for all

Whom once more I present unto your highness.

KING

And once more in mine arms I bid him welcome
98 And thank the holy conclave for their loves.
They have sent me such a man I would have wished
for.

CAMPEIUS

100 Your grace must needs deserve all strangers' loves,
You are so noble. To your highness' hand
I tender my commission, by whose virtue,
The court of Rome commanding, you, my Lord
Cardinal of York, are joined with me their servant
In the unpartial judging of this business.

KING

106 Two equal men. The queen shall be acquainted
Forthwith for what you come. Where's Gardiner?

WOLSEY

I know your majesty has always loved her
So dear in heart, not to deny her that
110 A woman of less place might ask by law –
Scholars allowed freely to argue for her.

KING

Ay, and the best she shall have; and my favor
To him that does best, God forbid else. Cardinal,
Prithee call Gardiner to me, my new secretary.
I find him a fit fellow.   *[Exit Wolsey.]*
     Enter [Wolsey, with] Gardiner.

WOLSEY   *[Aside to Gardiner]*

Give me your hand. Much joy and favor to you;
You are the king's now.

GARDINER   *[Aside to Wolsey]*

                    But to be commanded
For ever by your grace, whose hand has raised me.

---

98 *conclave* assembly of Catholic cardinals   **100** *strangers'* foreigners'   **106**
equal impartial   **110** *less place* lower rank

·KING
      Come hither, Gardiner.
      Walks and whispers.
CAMPEIUS
      My Lord of York, was not one Doctor Pace   120
      In this man's place before him?
WOLSEY   Yes, he was.
CAMPEIUS
      Was he not held a learned man?
WOLSEY   Yes, surely.
CAMPEIUS
      Believe me, there's an ill opinion spread then,
      Even of yourself, lord cardinal.
WOLSEY   How? Of me?
CAMPEIUS
      They will not stick to say you envied him,   125
      And fearing he would rise (he was so virtuous),
      Kept him a foreign man still, which so grieved him   127
      That he ran mad and died.
WOLSEY   Heav'n's peace be with him!
      That's Christian care enough. For living murmurers   129
      There's places of rebuke. He was a fool,   130
      For he would needs be virtuous. That good fellow,
      If I command him, follows my appointment;   132
      I will have none so near else. Learn this, brother,   133
      We live not to be griped by meaner persons.   134
KING
      Deliver this with modesty to th' queen. *Exit Gardiner.*   135
      The most convenient place that I can think of
      For such receipt of learning is Blackfriars.   137
      There ye shall meet about this weighty business.

---

125 *stick* scruple 127 *Kept . . . still* i.e., constantly employed him on foreign missions 129 *murmurers* grumblers 130 *places of rebuke* correctional
institutions 132 *appointment* directions 133 *near* familiar 134 *griped*
grasped by the hand; *meaner* lesser 135 *Deliver . . . modesty* inform the
queen without making too much of it 137 *receipt . . . learning* (1) receiving
learned men, (2) hearing learned discourses

139   My Wolsey, see it furnished. O my lord,
140   Would it not grieve an able man to leave
    So sweet a bedfellow? But conscience, conscience!
    O 'tis a tender place, and I must leave her.   *Exeunt.*

*

~ II.3 *Enter Anne Bullen and an Old Lady.*

ANNE
1   Not for that neither; here's the pang that pinches:
    His highness having lived so long with her, and she
    So good a lady that no tongue could ever
    Pronounce dishonor of her – by my life,
    She never knew harmdoing – O, now after
6   So many courses of the sun enthronèd,
7   Still growing in a majesty and pomp, the which
    To leave a thousandfold more bitter than
9   'Tis sweet at first t' acquire – after this process
10   To give her the avaunt, it is a pity
11   Would move a monster.

OLD LADY   Hearts of most hard temper
    Melt and lament for her.

ANNE   O God's will, much better
13   She ne'er had known pomp. Though't be temporal,
14   Yet if that quarrel, fortune, do divorce
15   It from the bearer, 'tis a sufferance panging
    As soul and body's severing.

OLD LADY   Alas, poor lady,
17   She's a stranger now again.

ANNE   So much the more
    Must pity drop upon her. Verily

---

139 *furnished* duly prepared
    II.3 The queen's apartments **1** *pinches* hurts **6** *courses . . . enthronèd*
years **7–8** *the which / To leave* to leave which **9** *process* proceeding **10**
avaunt dismissal **11** *temper* disposition **13** *temporal* earthly, transient **14**
quarrel troublemaker **15** *sufferance panging* painful suffering **17** *stranger*
foreigner

I swear 'tis better to be lowly born
And range with humble livers in content   20
Than to be perked up in a glist'ring grief   21
And wear a golden sorrow.
OLD LADY   Our content
Is our best having.   23
ANNE   By my troth and maidenhead,
I would not be a queen.   24
OLD LADY   Beshrew me, I would,
And venture maidenhead for't; and so would you,
For all this spice of your hypocrisy.   26
You that have so fair parts of women on you   27
Have, too, a woman's heart, which ever yet
Affected eminence, wealth, sovereignty;   29
Which, to say sooth, are blessings; and which gifts   30
(Saving your mincing) the capacity   31
Of your soft cheveril conscience would receive,   32
If you might please to stretch it.   33
ANNE   Nay, good troth.
OLD LADY
Yes troth, and troth. You would not be a queen?
ANNE
No, not for all the riches under heaven.
OLD LADY
'Tis strange. A threepence bowed would hire me,   36
Old as I am, to queen it. But I pray you,   37
What think you of a duchess? Have you limbs
To bear that load of title?
ANNE   No, in truth.

---

20 *range . . . livers* rank with humble people   21 *perked up in* uplifted into
23 *having* possession   24 *queen* (Anne's first use of this term sets up a series
of puns on "quean" as prostitute in the ensuing dialogue); *Beshrew me* woe
befall me   26 *spice* dash   27 *fair parts* attractive qualities   29 *Affected* desired   30 *to say sooth* to tell the truth   31 *mincing* hypocritical affectation
32 *cheveril* i.e., like soft, pliable leather   33, 34 *troth* faith (but punning on
"trot," old hag)   36 *bowed* bent, therefore worthless (with pun on "bawd")
37 *queen* (pun on "quean")

OLD LADY

40   Then you are weakly made. Pluck off a little;
41   I would not be a young count in your way
42   For more than blushing comes to. If your back
43   Cannot vouchsafe this burden, 'tis too weak
     Ever to get a boy.

ANNE   How you do talk!
     I swear again, I would not be a queen
46   For all the world.

OLD LADY   In faith, for little England
47   You'd venture an emballing. I myself
48   Would for Carnarvonshire, although there longed
     No more to th' crown but that. Lo, who comes here?
     Enter Lord Chamberlain.

CHAMBERLAIN

50   Good morrow, ladies. What were't worth to know
     The secret of your conference?

ANNE   My good lord,
52   Not your demand; it values not your asking.
     Our mistress' sorrows we were pitying.

CHAMBERLAIN
     It was a gentle business and becoming
     The action of good women. There is hope
     All will be well.

ANNE   Now I pray God, amen.

CHAMBERLAIN
     You bear a gentle mind, and heav'nly blessings
     Follow such creatures. That you may, fair lady,
     Perceive I speak sincerely, and high note's

---

40 *Pluck off* (1) come down a level, (2) remove the fancy dress   **41** *count* (an aristocratic rank, with possible pun on "cunt")   **42** *For . . . comes to* i.e., with (no) more fuss than a blush (i.e., she would yield herself quite happily)   **43** *vouchsafe* tolerate (i.e., bearing the weight of a man)   **46** *little England* (a term sometimes applied to Pembrokeshire, but also applicable to England as a whole)   **47** *an emballing* (1) being invested with the orb of royalty, (2) having sex (being balled)   **48** *Carnarvonshire* a barren county in Wales; *longed* belonged   **52** *Not . . . demand* don't ask

Ta'en of your many virtues, the king's majesty   60
Commends his good opinion of you, and   61
Does purpose honor to you no less flowing
Than Marchioness of Pembroke; to which title
A thousand pound a year, annual support,
Out of his grace he adds.
ANNE   I do not know
What kind of my obedience I should tender.
More than my all is nothing; nor my prayers   67
Are not words duly hallowed, nor my wishes
More worth than empty vanities; yet prayers and
    wishes
Are all I can return. Beseech your lordship,   70
Vouchsafe to speak my thanks and my obedience,   71
As from a blushing handmaid, to his highness,
Whose health and royalty I pray for.
CHAMBERLAIN   Lady,
I shall not fail t' approve the fair conceit   74
The king hath of you. *[Aside]* I have perused her well.
Beauty and honor in her are so mingled
That they have caught the king; and who knows yet
But from this lady may proceed a gem
To lighten all this isle. – I'll to the king   79
And say I spoke with you.   80
ANNE   My honored lord.
                        Exit Lord Chamberlain.

OLD LADY
Why, this it is! See, see,   81
I have been begging sixteen years in court
(Am yet a courtier beggarly) nor could   83
Come pat betwixt too early and too late   84
For any suit of pounds; and you (O fate!),   85

---

61 *Commends . . . you* sends his compliments 67–68 *nor . . . not* (double
negative for emphasis) 71 *Vouchsafe* be so kind as 74 *fair conceit* good
opinion 79 *lighten* light up 81 *this it is* this is how it goes 83 *beggarly*
poor 84 *Come pat* hit the right moment 85 *suit of pounds* petition for
money

A very fresh fish here – fie, fie, fie upon
87 This compelled fortune! – have your mouth filled up
Before you open it.
ANNE   This is strange to me.
OLD LADY
89 How tastes it? Is it bitter? Forty pence, no.
90 There was a lady once ('tis an old story)
That would not be a queen, that would she not,
92 For all the mud in Egypt. Have you heard it?
ANNE
93 Come, you are pleasant.
OLD LADY   With your theme I could
94 O'ermount the lark. The Marchioness of Pembroke?
A thousand pounds a year, for pure respect?
No other obligation? By my life,
97 That promises more thousands! Honor's train
Is longer than his foreskirt. By this time
I know your back will bear a duchess. Say,
100 Are you not stronger than you were?
ANNE   Good lady,
101 Make yourself mirth with your particular fancy
And leave me out on't. Would I had no being
103 If this salute my blood a jot! It faints me
To think what follows.
The queen is comfortless, and we forgetful
106 In our long absence. Pray do not deliver
What here y' have heard to her.
OLD LADY   What do you think me?
                                        Exeunt.

*

---

87 *compelled* i.e., thrust upon her   **89** *Forty pence, no* i.e., I'll bet you forty pence that it doesn't   **92** *mud in Egypt* i.e., the wealth of Egypt, based on the fertile Nile valley   **93** *pleasant* humorous   **94** *O'ermount* rise higher than   **101** *particular* private   **103** *salute . . . jot* i.e., excites me in the least; *faints me* makes me feel faint   **106** *deliver* make known

∾ **II.4** *Trumpets, sennet, and cornets.*
Enter two Vergers, with short silver wands; next them,
two Scribes, in the habit of doctors; after them, the
[Arch]bishop of Canterbury alone; after him, the
Bishops of Lincoln, Ely, Rochester, and Saint Asaph;
next them, with some small distance, follows a
Gentleman bearing the purse, with the great seal and a
cardinal's hat; then two Priests, bearing each a silver
cross; then [Griffith,] a Gentleman Usher, bareheaded,
accompanied with a Sergeant at Arms bearing a silver
mace; then two Gentlemen bearing two great silver
pillars; after them, side by side, the two Cardinals, two
Noblemen with the sword and mace. The King takes
place under the cloth of state; the two Cardinals sit
under him as Judges. The Queen takes place some
distance from the King. The Bishops place themselves
on each side the court, in manner of a consistory;
below them, the Scribes. The Lords sit next the Bishops.
The rest of the Attendants stand in convenient order
about the stage.

WOLSEY
  Whilst our commission from Rome is read,
  Let silence be commanded.
KING   What's the need?
  It hath already publicly been read,
  And on all sides th' authority allowed.   4
  You may then spare that time.
WOLSEY   Be't so. Proceed.

II.4 The court at Blackfriars s.d. *sennet* trumpet fanfare; *cornets* horns; *Vergers* officials who carry the symbols of office before dignitaries of the church or university; *Scribes* secretaries; *the habit of doctors* doctoral gowns and hoods; *silver pillars* (Wolsey's personal emblem, in addition to the silver mace to which he is entitled as a cardinal); *takes place* seats himself; *consistory* council chamber   4 *allowed* acknowledged

SCRIBE
Say, "Henry King of England, come into the court."
CRIER
Henry King of England, etc.
KING
Here.
SCRIBE
Say, "Katherine Queen of England, come into the
court."
CRIER
10   Katherine Queen of England, etc.

The Queen makes no answer, rises out of her chair,
goes about the court, comes to the King, and kneels at
his feet; then speaks.

[KATHERINE]
Sir, I desire you do me right and justice,
And to bestow your pity on me; for
13   I am a most poor woman and a stranger,
Born out of your dominions: having here
15   No judge indifferent, nor no more assurance
16   Of equal friendship and proceeding. Alas, sir,
In what have I offended you? What cause
Hath my behavior given to your displeasure
19   That thus you should proceed to put me off
20   And take your good grace from me? Heaven witness,
I have been to you a true and humble wife,
22   At all times to your will conformable,
Ever in fear to kindle your dislike,
Yea, subject to your countenance, glad or sorry
As I saw it inclined. When was the hour
I ever contradicted your desire
Or made it not mine too? Or which of your friends
Have I not strove to love, although I knew
He were mine enemy? What friend of mine

---

13 *stranger* foreigner   15 *indifferent* impartial   16 *equal* fair   19 *put me off*
discard me   20 *good grace* favor and person   22 *conformable* conforming

That had to him derived your anger, did I   30
Continue in my liking? Nay, gave notice
He was from thence discharged? Sir, call to mind
That I have been your wife in this obedience
Upward of twenty years, and have been blessed
With many children by you. If in the course
And process of this time you can report,
And prove it too, against mine honor aught,
My bond to wedlock, or my love and duty
Against your sacred person, in God's name   39
Turn me away, and let the foul'st contempt   40
Shut door upon me, and so give me up
To the sharp'st kind of justice. Please you, sir,
The king your father was reputed for
A prince most prudent, of an excellent
And unmatched wit and judgment. Ferdinand,   45
My father, King of Spain, was reckoned one   46
The wisest prince that there had reigned by many
A year before. It is not to be questioned
That they had gathered a wise council to them
Of every realm, that did debate this business,   50
Who deemed our marriage lawful. Wherefore I humbly
Beseech you, sir, to spare me till I may
Be by my friends in Spain advised, whose counsel
I will implore. If not, i' th' name of God,
Your pleasure be fulfilled!
WOLSEY   You have here, lady
  (And of your choice), these reverend fathers, men
  Of singular integrity and learning,
  Yea, the elect o' th' land, who are assembled
  To plead your cause. It shall be therefore bootless   59
  That longer you desire the court, as well   60
  For your own quiet as to rectify

---

30 *derived* attracted 39 *Against* toward 45 *unmatched* incomparable; *wit*
wisdom 46 *one* one of 59 *bootless* fruitless 60 *desire* i.e., to delay the
business

What is unsettled in the king.
CAMPEIUS   His grace
Hath spoken well and justly. Therefore, madam,
It's fit this royal session do proceed
And that without delay their arguments
Be now produced and heard.
KATHERINE   Lord cardinal,
To you I speak.
WOLSEY   Your pleasure, madam.
KATHERINE   Sir,
I am about to weep; but, thinking that

69   We are a queen (or long have dreamed so), certain
70   The daughter of a king, my drops of tears
I'll turn to sparks of fire.
WOLSEY   Be patient yet.
KATHERINE
I will, when you are humble; nay before,
Or God will punish me. I do believe

74   (Induced by potent circumstances) that
75   You are mine enemy, and make my challenge,
You shall not be my judge. For it is you

77   Have blown this coal betwixt my lord and me,
Which God's dew quench! Therefore I say again

79   I utterly abhor, yea, from my soul
80   Refuse you for my judge, whom yet once more
I hold my most malicious foe and think not

82   At all a friend to truth.
WOLSEY   I do profess
You speak not like yourself, who ever yet

84   Have stood to charity and displayed th' effects
Of disposition gentle, and of wisdom
O'ertopping woman's pow'r. Madam, you do me
wrong.

---

69 *certain* certainly   74 *Induced* persuaded   75 *challenge* legal objection
77 *blown this coal* i.e., created this strife   79 *abhor* protest, reject   82 *profess*
affirm   84 *stood to* upheld

I have no spleen against you, nor injustice   87
For you or any. How far I have proceeded,
Or how far further shall, is warranted
By a commission from the consistory,   90
Yea, the whole consistory of Rome. You charge me
That I have blown this coal: I do deny it.
The king is present. If it be known to him
That I gainsay my deed, how may he wound,   94
And worthily, my falsehood, yea, as much   95
As you have done my truth. If he know
That I am free of your report, he knows   97
I am not of your wrong. Therefore in him   98
It lies to cure me, and the cure is to
Remove these thoughts from you; the which before   100
His highness shall speak in, I do beseech   101
You, gracious madam, to unthink your speaking
And to say so no more.
KATHERINE   My lord, my lord,
I am a simple woman, much too weak
T' oppose your cunning. You're meek and humble-
    mouthed;
You sign your place and calling, in full seeming,   106
With meekness and humility, but your heart
Is crammed with arrogancy, spleen, and pride.   108
You have, by fortune and his highness' favors,
Gone slightly o'er low steps, and now are mounted   110
Where pow'rs are your retainers, and your words   111
(Domestics to you) serve your will as't please
Yourself pronounce their office. I must tell you
You tender more your person's honor than   114

---

87 *spleen* anger 90 *consistory* assembly of cardinals 94 *gainsay my deed*
deny what I have done 95 *worthily* deservedly 97 *free of your report* innocent of your charge 98 *I . . . wrong* i.e., I have done nothing to injure you
101 *in* in reference to 106 *sign your place* signify your office 108 *spleen*
anger, malice 110 *slightly* easily 111 *pow'rs* powerful people 111–13
your words . . . office i.e., your words are immediately acted upon, as if they
were your servants 114 *tender* cherish

Your high profession spiritual; that again
I do refuse you for my judge and here,
Before you all, appeal unto the pope,
To bring my whole cause 'fore his holiness
119   And to be judged by him.
       She curtsies to the King and offers to depart.
CAMPEIUS   The queen is obstinate,
120   Stubborn to justice, apt to accuse it, and
       Disdainful to be tried by't. 'Tis not well.
       She's going away.
KING
       Call her again.
CRIER
       Katherine Queen of England, come into the court.
GRIFFITH
       Madam, you are called back.
KATHERINE
126   What need you note it? Pray you keep your way;
       When you are called, return. Now the Lord help,
       They vex me past my patience. Pray you pass on.
       I will not tarry; no, nor ever more
130 Upon this business my appearance make
       In any of their courts. *Exeunt Queen and her Attendants.*
KING   Go thy ways, Kate.
       That man i' th' world who shall report he has
       A better wife, let him in nought be trusted
       For speaking false in that. Thou art alone
135   (If thy rare qualities, sweet gentleness,
136   Thy meekness saintlike, wifelike government,
137   Obeying in commanding, and thy parts
138   Sovereign and pious else, could speak thee out)
       The queen of earthly queens. She's noble born,
140 And like her true nobility she has

---

119 s.d. *offers* ventures   **120** *Stubborn to* resistant to   **126** *keep your way*
keep on your way   **135** *rare* excelling   **136** *government* self-control   **137**
parts qualities   **138** *speak thee out* accurately describe you

Carried herself towards me.   141
WOLSEY   Most gracious sir,
In humblest manner I require your highness   142
That it shall please you to declare in hearing
Of all these ears (for where I am robbed and bound
There must I be unloosed, although not there
At once and fully satisfied) whether ever I   146
Did broach this business to your highness, or
Laid any scruple in your way which might
Induce you to the question on't; or ever   149
Have to you, but with thanks to God for such   *150*
A royal lady, spake one the least word that might   151
Be to the prejudice of her present state   152
Or touch of her good person.   153
KING   My lord cardinal,
I do excuse you; yea, upon mine honor,   154
I free you from't. You are not to be taught
That you have many enemies that know not
Why they are so, but like to village curs
Bark when their fellows do. By some of these
The queen is put in anger. You're excused.
But will you be more justified? You ever   *160*
Have wished the sleeping of this business; never desired
It to be stirred, but oft have hindered, oft
The passages made toward it. On my honor,   163
I speak my good lord card'nal to this point,
And thus far clear him. Now what moved me to't,
I will be bold with time and your attention:
Then mark th' inducement. Thus it came; give heed   167
to't:
My conscience first received a tenderness,
Scruple and prick, on certain speeches uttered

---

141 *Carried* conducted   142 *require* request   146 *satisfied* given satisfaction
149 *to the question on't* i.e., to take up the issue   151 *one the least* the least
152 *prejudice* detriment   153 *touch* sullying   154 *excuse* exculpate   163
passages proceedings   167 *inducement* instigation

170 By th' Bishop of Bayonne, then French ambassador,
Who had been hither sent on the debating
A marriage 'twixt the Duke of Orleans and
Our daughter Mary. I' th' progress of this business,
174 Ere a determinate resolution, he
175 (I mean the bishop) did require a respite,
176 Wherein he might the king his lord advertise
Whether our daughter were legitimate,
Respecting this our marriage with the dowager,
179 Sometimes our brother's wife. This respite shook
180 The bosom of my conscience, entered me,
181 Yea, with a spitting power, and made to tremble
The region of my breast, which forced such way
183 That many mazed considerings did throng
And pressed in with this caution. First, methought
185 I stood not in the smile of heaven, who had
Commanded nature that my lady's womb,
If it conceived a male child by me, should
188 Do no more offices of life to't than
The grave does to th' dead; for her male issue
190 Or died where they were made or shortly after
191 This world had aired them. Hence I took a thought
This was a judgment on me, that my kingdom
(Well worthy the best heir o' th' world) should not
Be gladded in't by me. Then follows that
I weighed the danger which my realms stood in
196 By this my issue's fail, and that gave to me
197 Many a groaning throe. Thus hulling in
The wild sea of my conscience, I did steer

---

174 *determinate resolution* final settlement   175 *require a respite* request a
delay   176 *advertise* inform   179 *Sometimes* formerly (Katherine had previously been married to Henry's elder brother Arthur, the heir apparent, who
had died, as a result of which Henry became king and married Katherine)
181 *spitting* piercing   183 *mazed* perplexed   185 *smile* good graces   188
offices services   190 *Or . . . or* either . . . or   191 *aired them* given them
breath   196 *issue's fail* failure to produce (male) heirs   197 *throe* fit of an-
guish; *hulling* adrift

Toward this remedy whereupon we are
Now present here together. That's to say   *200*
I mean to rectify my conscience, which   201
I then did feel full sick, and yet not well,   202
By all the reverend fathers of the land
And doctors learned. First I began in private   204
With you, my Lord of Lincoln. You remember
How under my oppression I did reek   206
When I first moved you.
LINCOLN   Very well, my liege.
KING
I have spoke long. Be pleased yourself to say
How far you satisfied me.
LINCOLN   So please your highness,
The question did at first so stagger me,   *210*
Bearing a state of mighty moment in't   211
And consequence of dread, that I committed   212
The daring'st counsel which I had to doubt
And did entreat your highness to this course
Which you are running here.
KING   I then moved you,
My Lord of Canterbury, and got your leave
To make this present summons. Unsolicited
I left no reverend person in this court,
But by particular consent proceeded
Under your hands and seals. Therefore go on,   220
For no dislike i' th' world against the person
Of the good queen, but the sharp thorny points
Of my allegèd reasons, drives this forward.   223
Prove but our marriage lawful, by my life
And kingly dignity, we are contented

---

201 *rectify* clear, set right   202 *yet* still   204 *doctors* lawyers, scholars   206 *oppression* distress; *reek* sweat   207 *moved* appealed to   211 *Bearing . . . moment* concerning a situation of great importance   212 *consequence of dread* fearful outcome   212–13 *committed . . . to doubt* i.e., gave, although doubtfully, my boldest advice   220 *Under . . . seals* with your written and signed consent   223 *allegèd* already stated

226 To wear our mortal state to come with her,
     Katherine our queen, before the primest creature
228 That's paragoned o' th' world.
     CAMPEIUS   So please your highness,
     The queen being absent, 'tis a needful fitness
230 That we adjourn this court till further day.
231 Meanwhile must be an earnest motion
     Made to the queen to call back her appeal
     She intends unto his holiness.
     KING   *[Aside]*   I may perceive
     These cardinals trifle with me. I abhor
     This dilatory sloth and tricks of Rome.
     My learned and well-belovèd servant Cranmer,
     Prithee return. With thy approach I know
     My comfort comes along. – Break up the court;
     I say set on.   *Exeunt, in manner as they entered.*
                              ✳

∾ III.1 *Enter the Queen and her Women, as at work.*

KATHERINE
     Take thy lute, wench, my soul grows sad with troubles;
2   Sing, and disperse 'em if thou canst. Leave working.
                         Song.
          Orpheus with his lute made trees,
          And the mountain tops that freeze,
             Bow themselves when he did sing.
          To his music plants and flowers
7   Ever sprung, as sun and showers
             There had made a lasting spring.

          Every thing that heard him play,
10   Even the billows of the sea,

---

226 *mortal state* i.e., garb and appurtenances of kingship 228 *paragoned*
held up as model of excellence 230 *further day* a future date 231 *motion*
plea
      III.1 The queen's apartments 2 *Leave* cease 7 *as* as if

    Hung their heads, and then lay by.   11
    In sweet music is such art,
      Killing care and grief of heart
      Fall asleep, or hearing die.
  Enter a Gentleman.

KATHERINE
  How now?

GENTLEMAN
  An't please your grace, the two great cardinals   16
  Wait in the presence.   17

KATHERINE   Would they speak with me?

GENTLEMAN
  They willed me say so, madam.   18

KATHERINE   Pray their graces
  To come near.   *[Exit Gentleman.]*
          What can be their business
  With me, a poor weak woman, fall'n from favor?   20
  I do not like their coming. Now I think on't,
  They should be good men, their affairs as righteous, 22
  But all hoods make not monks.
  Enter the two Cardinals, Wolsey and Campeius.

WOLSEY   Peace to your highness.

KATHERINE
  Your graces find me here part of a housewife
  (I would be all) against the worst may happen.   25
  What are your pleasures with me, reverend lords?

WOLSEY
  May it please you, noble madam, to withdraw
  Into your private chamber, we shall give you
  The full cause of our coming.

KATHERINE   Speak it here.
  There's nothing I have done yet, o' my conscience, 30
  Deserves a corner. Would all other women   31

---

11 *lay by* rested 16 *An't* if it 17 *presence* presence chamber 18 *willed* requested 22 *affairs* business 25 *would be* wish I were; *against* in preparation for 31 *a corner* i.e., secrecy

32   Could speak this with as free a soul as I do!
       My lords, I care not (so much I am happy
34   Above a number) if my actions
       Were tried by ev'ry tongue, ev'ry eye saw 'em,
36   Envy and base opinion set against 'em,
37   I know my life so even. If your business
38   Seek me out, and that way I am wife in,
       Out with it boldly: truth loves open dealing.
40 WOLSEY   *Tanta est erga te mentis integritas, regina serenis-*
       sima —
       KATHERINE
       O, good my lord, no Latin!
43   I am not such a truant since my coming
       As not to know the language I have lived in.
45   A strange tongue makes my cause more strange, suspi-
       cious.
       Pray speak in English. Here are some will thank you,
       If you speak truth, for their poor mistress' sake.
       Believe me, she has had much wrong. Lord cardinal,
49   The willing'st sin I ever yet committed
50   May be absolved in English.
       WOLSEY   Noble lady,
       I am sorry my integrity should breed
       (And service to his majesty and you)
53   So deep suspicion where all faith was meant.
54   We come not by the way of accusation
       To taint that honor every good tongue blesses,
56   Nor to betray you any way to sorrow —
       You have too much, good lady — but to know
       How you stand minded in the weighty difference

---

32 *free* innocent 34 *a number* many 36 *Envy* malice; *opinion* gossip 37 *even* constant (in its uprightness) 38 *that way I am wife in* i.e., pertaining to my situation as a wife 40–41 *Tanta . . . serenissima* such is the honesty of my mind toward you,, O most serene queen 43 *truant* idler 45 *strange . . . strange* foreign . . . unfamiliar 49 *willing'st* most deliberate 53 *faith* loyalty 54 *by the way . . . accusation* in order to accuse you 56 *any way* in any manner

Between the king and you, and to deliver   59
(Like free and honest men) our just opinions   60
And comforts to your cause.
CAMPEIUS   Most honored madam,
My Lord of York, out of his noble nature,
Zeal and obedience he still bore your grace,   63
Forgetting (like a good man) your late censure
Both of his truth and him (which was too far),   65
Offers, as I do, in a sign of peace,   66
His service and his counsel.
KATHERINE   *[Aside]*   To betray me. –
My lords, I thank you both for your good wills,
Ye speak like honest men (pray God ye prove so).
But how to make ye suddenly an answer   70
In such a point of weight, so near mine honor   71
(More near my life, I fear), with my weak wit,   72
And to such men of gravity and learning,
In truth I know not. I was set at work   74
Among my maids, full little (God knows) looking
Either for such men or such business.
For her sake that I have been – for I feel
The last fit of my greatness – good your graces,   78
Let me have time and counsel for my cause.
Alas, I am a woman friendless, hopeless.   80
WOLSEY
Madam, you wrong the king's love with these fears.
Your hopes and friends are infinite.
KATHERINE   In England
But little for my profit. Can you think, lords,
That any Englishman dare give me counsel?
Or be a known friend 'gainst his highness' pleasure
(Though he be grown so desperate to be honest)   86

---

59 *deliver* convey 60 *honest* honorable 63 *still* always 65 *was* went 66
in a sign as a token 70 *suddenly* on the spur of the moment 71 *near* inti-
mately affecting 72 *wit* understanding 74 *set* seated 78 *last fit* death
spasm 86 *so desperate . . . honest* so reckless as to tell the truth

And live a subject? Nay forsooth, my friends,
88 They that must weigh out my afflictions,
They that my trust must grow to, live not here.
90 They are (as all my other comforts) far hence
In mine own country, lords.
CAMPEIUS   I would your grace
Would leave your griefs and take my counsel.
KATHERINE   How, sir?
CAMPEIUS
Put your main cause into the king's protection,
He's loving and most gracious. 'Twill be much
Both for your honor better and your cause;
For if the trial of the law o'ertake ye,
97 You'll part away disgraced.
WOLSEY   He tells you rightly.
KATHERINE
Ye tell me what ye wish for both – my ruin.
Is this your Christian counsel? Out upon ye!
100 Heaven is above all yet; there sits a judge
101 That no king can corrupt.
CAMPEIUS   Your rage mistakes us.
KATHERINE
The more shame for ye! Holy men I thought ye,
103 Upon my soul, two reverend cardinal virtues;
But cardinal sins and hollow hearts I fear ye.
Mend 'em for shame, my lords! Is this your comfort?
106 The cordial that ye bring a wretched lady?
107 A woman lost among ye, laughed at, scorned?
I will not wish ye half my miseries,
I have more charity. But say I warned ye.
110 Take heed, for heaven's sake take heed, lest at once
The burden of my sorrows fall upon ye.

---

88 *weigh out* (1) justly measure (?), (2) help to carry the weight of **97** *part
away* leave **101** *mistakes* misconstrues **103** *two reverend cardinal virtues*
i.e., two embodiments of the cardinal virtues faith, hope, and charity (punning on *cardinal,* as in the following line) **106** *cordial* restorative **107** *lost*
brought to ruin **110** *at once* all at once

WOLSEY
Madam, this is a mere distraction.   112
You turn the good we offer into envy.   113
KATHERINE
Ye turn me into nothing. Woe upon ye
And all such false professors! Would you have me   115
(If you have any justice, any pity,
If ye be anything but churchmen's habits)   117
Put my sick cause into his hands that hates me?
Alas, has banished me his bed already,   119
His love, too long ago. I am old, my lords,   *120*
And all the fellowship I hold now with him
Is only my obedience. What can happen
To me above this wretchedness? All your studies   123
Make me accursed like this.   124
CAMPEIUS   Your fears are worse.
KATHERINE
Have I lived thus long (let me speak myself,
Since virtue finds no friends) a wife, a true one?
A woman (I dare say without vainglory)
Never yet branded with suspicion?
Have I with all my full affections   129
Still met the king? Loved him next heav'n? Obeyed him?   130
Been (out of fondness) superstitious to him?   131
Almost forgot my prayers to content him?
And am I thus rewarded? 'Tis not well, lords.
Bring me a constant woman to her husband,   134
One that ne'er dreamed a joy beyond his pleasure,
And to that woman (when she has done most)
Yet will I add an honor – a great patience.
WOLSEY
Madam, you wander from the good we aim at.

---

112 *distraction* frenzy   113 *envy* malice   115 *professors* those who profess to
do, or be, good   117 *habits* outer garments   119 *has* he has   123 *studies* efforts   124 *accursed* afflicted, as if under a curse   129 *affections* love   130
Still always   131 *superstitious* excessively devoted   134 *constant woman to*
woman constant to

KATHERINE
    My lord, I dare not make myself so guilty
140   To give up willingly that noble title
    Your master wed me to. Nothing but death
    Shall e'er divorce my dignities.
WOLSEY   Pray hear me.
KATHERINE
    Would I had never trod this English earth
    Or felt the flatteries that grow upon it!
    Ye have angels' faces, but heaven knows your hearts.
    What will become of me now, wretched lady?
    I am the most unhappy woman living.
       [To her Women]
    Alas, poor wenches, where are now your fortunes?
    Shipwracked upon a kingdom where no pity,
150   No friends, no hope, no kindred weep for me,
    Almost no grave allowed me. Like the lily
    That once was mistress of the field and flourished,
    I'll hang my head and perish.
WOLSEY   If your grace
154   Could but be brought to know our ends are honest,
    You'd feel more comfort. Why should we, good lady,
156   Upon what cause, wrong you? Alas, our places,
    The way of our profession is against it.
    We are to cure such sorrows, not to sow 'em.
    For goodness' sake, consider what you do,
160   How you may hurt yourself, ay, utterly
161   Grow from the king's acquaintance by this carriage.
    The hearts of princes kiss obedience,
    So much they love it; but to stubborn spirits
    They swell and grow as terrible as storms.
165   I know you have a gentle, noble temper,
    A soul as even as a calm. Pray think us
    Those we profess, peacemakers, friends, and servants.

---

154 *honest* honorable   **156** *places* (religious) offices   **161** *Grow from* become estranged from; *carriage* behavior   **165** *temper* disposition

CAMPEIUS
    Madam, you'll find it so. You wrong your virtues
    With these weak women's fears. A noble spirit,
    As yours was put into you, ever casts   170
    Such doubts as false coin from it. The king loves you:
    Beware you lose it not. For us, if you please
    To trust us in your business, we are ready
    To use our utmost studies in your service.   174
KATHERINE
    Do what ye will, my lords, and pray forgive me,
    If I have used myself unmannerly.   176
    You know I am a woman, lacking wit   177
    To make a seemly answer to such persons.
    Pray do my service to his majesty,   179
    He has my heart yet, and shall have my prayers   *180*
    While I shall have my life. Come, reverend fathers,
    Bestow your counsels on me. She now begs
    That little thought, when she set footing here,
    She should have bought her dignities so dear.   *Exeunt.*

                    *

∾ **III.2** *Enter the Duke of Norfolk, Duke of Suffolk,*
    Lord Surrey, and Lord Chamberlain.

NORFOLK
    If you will now unite in your complaints
    And force them with a constancy, the cardinal   2
    Cannot stand under them. If you omit   3
    The offer of this time, I cannot promise
    But that you shall sustain more new disgraces
    With these you bear already.
SURREY   I am joyful

---

170 *As . . . put into* i.e., such as you were endowed with   174 *studies* efforts
176 *used myself* behaved   177 *wit* (masculine) understanding   179 *do my
service* pay my respects
    III.2 The king's apartments   2 *force . . . constancy* press them home with
persistence   3 *stand under* withstand; *omit* neglect

To meet the least occasion that may give me
8   Remembrance of my father-in-law, the duke,
To be revenged on him.
SUFFOLK   Which of the peers
10   Have uncontemned gone by him, or at least
Strangely neglected? When did he regard
The stamp of nobleness in any person
13   Out of himself?
CHAMBERLAIN   My lords, you speak your pleasures.
What he deserves of you and me I know.
What we can do to him (though now the time
16   Gives way to us) I much fear. If you cannot
17   Bar his access to th' king, never attempt
Anything on him; for he hath a witchcraft
Over the king in's tongue.
NORFOLK   O fear him not,
20   His spell in that is out. The king hath found
Matter against him that for ever mars
22   The honey of his language. No, he's settled
23   (Not to come off) in his displeasure.
SURREY   Sir,
I should be glad to hear such news as this
Once every hour.
NORFOLK   Believe it, this is true.
26   In the divorce his contrary proceedings
27   Are all unfolded; wherein he appears
As I would wish mine enemy.
SURREY   How came
29   His practices to light?
SUFFOLK   Most strangely.
SURREY   O how? How?

---

8 *the duke* i.e., Buckingham 10 *uncontemned* without being despised 13 *Out of* apart from 16 *Gives way to* favors 17–18 *attempt / Anything* make any attack 20 *His spell . . . out* i.e., his magical power of persuasion is exhausted 22 *settled* fixed 23 *his* i.e., the king's 26 *contrary* contradictory 27 *unfolded* revealed 29 *practices* intrigues

SUFFOLK
    The cardinal's letters to the pope miscarried   30
    And came to th' eye o' th' king, wherein was read
    How that the cardinal did entreat his holiness
    To stay the judgment o' th' divorce; for if
    It did take place, "I do," quoth he, "perceive
    My king is tangled in affection to
    A creature of the queen's, Lady Anne Bullen."   36
SURREY
    Has the king this?
SUFFOLK   Believe it.
SURREY   Will this work?
CHAMBERLAIN
    The king in this perceives him, how he coasts   38
    And hedges his own way. But in this point   39
    All his tricks founder and he brings his physic   40
    After his patient's death: the king already
    Hath married the fair lady.
SURREY   Would he had!
SUFFOLK
    May you be happy in your wish, my lord,
    For I profess you have it.   44
SURREY   Now all my joy
    Trace the conjunction!   45
SUFFOLK   My amen to't!
NORFOLK   All men's!
SUFFOLK
    There's order given for her coronation.
    Marry this is yet but young, and may be left   47
    To some ears unrecounted. But, my lords,
    She is a gallant creature and complete   49
    In mind and feature. I persuade me, from her   50

---

30 *miscarried* went astray   36 *creature* minion, agent   38 *coasts* maneuvers
circuitously   39 *hedges . . . way* dodges around for his own ends   40
founder sink, come to nought; *physic* medicine   44 *profess* declare   45 *Trace*
follow, attend upon; *conjunction* union, marriage   47 *Marry* to be sure ("by
Mary"); *young* new   49 *gallant* splendid; *complete* perfect

Will fall some blessing to this land, which shall
52   In it be memorized.
SURREY   But will the king
53   Digest this letter of the cardinal's?
  The Lord forbid!
NORFOLK   Marry amen.
SUFFOLK   No, no;
  There be more wasps that buzz about his nose
  Will make this sting the sooner. Cardinal Campeius
  Is stol'n away to Rome, hath ta'en no leave,
  Has left the cause o' th' king unhandled, and
59   Is posted as the agent of our cardinal
60   To second all his plot. I do assure you
61   The king cried "Ha" at this.
CHAMBERLAIN   Now God incense him
  And let him cry "Ha" louder!
NORFOLK   But, my lord,
  When returns Cranmer?
SUFFOLK
64   He is returned in his opinions, which
  Have satisfied the king for his divorce,
  Together with all famous colleges
  Almost in Christendom. Shortly, I believe,
68   His second marriage shall be published and
  Her coronation. Katherine no more
70   Shall be called queen, but princess dowager,
  And widow to Prince Arthur.
NORFOLK   This same Cranmer's
72   A worthy fellow, and hath ta'en much pain
  In the king's business.
SUFFOLK   He has, and we shall see him
  For it an archbishop.

---

52 *memorized* memorialized, long remembered   53 *Digest* i.e., "stomach,"
tolerate   59 *Is posted* has gone posthaste   61 *Ha* (the king's favorite exclamation)   64 *is . . . opinions* (1) is of the same opinion as before (?), (2) has
gathered opinions abroad in support of the king's position (?)   68 *published*
announced   72 *pain* i.e., pains

NORFOLK   So I hear.
SUFFOLK   'Tis so.
    Enter Wolsey and Cromwell.
    The cardinal!
NORFOLK   Observe, observe, he's moody.
WOLSEY
    The packet, Cromwell,
    Gave't you the king?
CROMWELL   To his own hand, in's bedchamber.
WOLSEY
    Looked he o' th' inside of the paper?   78
CROMWELL   Presently
    He did unseal them, and the first he viewed,
    He did it with a serious mind; a heed   80
    Was in his countenance. You he bade
    Attend him here this morning.
WOLSEY   Is he ready
    To come abroad?
CROMWELL   I think by this he is.
WOLSEY
    Leave me awhile.   *Exit Cromwell.*
    [Aside]
    It shall be to the Duchess of Alençon,
    The French king's sister; he shall marry her.
    Anne Bullen? No! I'll no Anne Bullens for him;
    There's more in't than fair visage. Bullen?
    No, we'll no Bullens! Speedily I wish
    To hear from Rome. The Marchioness of Pembroke?   90
NORFOLK
    He's discontented.
SUFFOLK   May be he hears the king
    Does whet his anger to him.
SURREY   Sharp enough,
    Lord, for thy justice!

_____

78 *paper* wrapper

WOLSEY *[Aside]*
  The late queen's gentlewoman? A knight's daughter
  To be her mistress' mistress? The queen's queen?
  This candle burns not clear, 'tis I must snuff it,
  Then out it goes. What though I know her virtuous
  And well-deserving? Yet I know her for
99   A spleeny Lutheran, and not wholesome to
100   Our cause that she should lie i' th' bosom of
101   Our hard-ruled king. Again there is sprung up
102   An heretic, an arch one – Cranmer – one
103   Hath crawled into the favor of the king
104   And is his oracle.
NORFOLK   He is vexed at something.
  Enter King, reading of a schedule [, and Lovell].
SURREY
105   I would 'twere something that would fret the string,
106   The master cord on's heart.
SUFFOLK   The king, the king!
KING
  What piles of wealth hath he accumulated
108   To his own portion! And what expense by th' hour
  Seems to flow from him! How i' th' name of thrift
110   Does he rake this together? – Now, my lords,
  Saw you the cardinal?
NORFOLK   My lord, we have
112   Stood here observing him. Some strange commotion
  Is in his brain. He bites his lip, and starts,
  Stops on a sudden, looks upon the ground,
  Then lays his finger on his temple; straight
  Springs out into fast gait, then stops again,

---

99 *spleeny* passionate; *wholesome* beneficial (*Our cause,* l. 100, being both Wolsey's own and that of the Catholic church)   **100** *lie i' th' bosom of* (1) be the confidante of, (2) be married to   **101** *hard-ruled* hard-to-manage   **102** *arch* chief   **103** *Hath* who has   **104** *oracle* i.e., most influential counselor; **s.d.** *schedule* scroll   **105** *fret the string* corrode (with pun on the "fret" of a stringed instrument)   **106** *on's* of his   **108** *portion* share; *expense* prodigal expenditure   **112** *commotion* upset

Strikes his breast hard, and anon he casts
His eye against the moon. In most strange postures   118
We have seen him set himself.
KING   It may well be,
  There is a mutiny in's mind. This morning   120
  Papers of state he sent me to peruse
  As I required, and wot you what I found   122
  There, on my conscience, put unwittingly?
  Forsooth an inventory, thus importing   124
  The several parcels of his plate, his treasure,   125
  Rich stuffs and ornaments of household, which
  I find at such proud rate that it outspeaks   127
  Possession of a subject.
NORFOLK   It's heaven's will.
  Some spirit put this paper in the packet
  To bless your eye withal.   130
KING   If we did think
  His contemplation were above the earth
  And fixed on spiritual object, he should still
  Dwell in his musings; but I am afraid
  His thinkings are below the moon, not worth   134
  His serious considering.
    King takes his seat; whispers [to] Lovell, who goes to
    the Cardinal.
WOLSEY   Heaven forgive me;
  Even God bless your highness!
KING   Good my lord,
  You are full of heavenly stuff, and bear the inventory   137
  Of your best graces in your mind; the which
  You were now running o'er. You have scarce time
  To steal from spiritual leisure a brief span   140
  To keep your earthly audit. Sure in that

---

118 *against* toward   122 *wot* know   124 *importing* indicating   125 *several*
parcels separate items   127–28 *outspeaks . . . subject* enumerates more than is
appropriate for a subject to own   130 *withal* therewith   134 *below the*
moon worldly   137 *stuff* goods   140 *spiritual leisure* time devoted to religious duties or reflections

142   I deem you an ill husband, and am glad
      To have you therein my companion.
     WOLSEY   Sir,
      For holy offices I have a time; a time
      To think upon the part of business which
      I bear i' th' state; and nature does require
147   Her times of preservation, which perforce
      I, her frail son, amongst my brethren mortal,
149   Must give my tendance to.
     KING   You have said well.
     WOLSEY
150   And ever may your highness yoke together
      (As I will lend you cause) my doing well
      With my well saying!
     KING   'Tis well said again,
      And 'tis a kind of good deed to say well;
      And yet words are no deeds. My father loved you;
155   He said he did, and with his deed did crown
      His word upon you. Since I had my office,
      I have kept you next my heart; have not alone
      Employed you where high profits might come home,
159   But pared my present havings to bestow
160   My bounties upon you.
     WOLSEY *[Aside]*   What should this mean?
     SURREY *[Aside]*
      The Lord increase this business!
     KING   Have I not made you
162   The prime man of the state? I pray you tell me
163   If what I now pronounce you have found true.
164   And if you may confess it, say withal
      If you are bound to us or no. What say you?

---

142 *ill husband* bad manager   147 *preservation* i.e., rest and recovery   149 *tendance* attention   155 *crown* i.e., nobly fulfill   159 *pared* skimped (like paring the cheese down to the rind); *havings* possessions   162 *prime* principal   163 *pronounce* declare   164 *withal* in addition

WOLSEY
   My sovereign, I confess your royal graces,
   Showered on me daily, have been more than could
   My studied purposes requite, which went   168
   Beyond all man's endeavors. My endeavors
   Have ever come too short of my desires,   170
   Yet filled with my abilities. Mine own ends   171
   Have been mine so, that evermore they pointed   172
   To th' good of your most sacred person and
   The profit of the state. For your great graces
·   Heaped upon me (poor undeserver) I
   Can nothing render but allegiant thanks,
   My prayers to heaven for you, my loyalty,
   Which ever has and ever shall be growing,
   Till death (that winter) kill it.   179
KING   Fairly answered:
   A loyal and obedient subject is   180
   Therein illustrated. The honor of it   181
   Does pay the act of it, as i' th' contrary
   The foulness is the punishment. I presume   183
   That, as my hand has opened bounty to you,   184
   My heart dropped love, my pow'r rained honor, more
   On you than any, so your hand and heart,
   Your brain and every function of your power
   Should, notwithstanding that your bond of duty,   188
   As 'twere in love's particular, be more   189
   To me, your friend, than any.   190
WOLSEY   I do profess
   That for your highness' good I ever labored

---

168 *studied purposes* deliberate efforts   171 *filled . . . abilities* i.e., conducted
to the best of my ability   172 *so* in such a way   179 *Fairly* finely, deferen-
tially   181–82 *The honor . . . it* the honor of being loyal is the reward of loyalty   183 *foulness* i.e., shameful blot   184 *opened* generously made available
188 *that* i.e., that particular thing; *bond . . . duty* (Wolsey's obligation to the
pope)   189 *particular* i.e., special intimacy and obligation

192 More than mine own; that am, have, and will be –
Though all the world should crack their duty to you
And throw it from their soul; though perils did
Abound as thick as thought could make 'em and
Appear in forms more horrid – yet my duty,
197 As doth a rock against the chiding flood,
198 Should the approach of this wild river break,
And stand unshaken yours.

KING   'Tis nobly spoken.
200 Take notice, lords, he has a loyal breast,
For you have seen him open't. Read o'er this,
        [Gives him papers.]
And after, this, and then to breakfast with
What appetite you have.
                    Exit King frowning upon the Cardinal.
        The Nobles throng after him, smiling and whispering.
WOLSEY   What should this mean?
What sudden anger's this? How have I reaped it?
He parted frowning from me, as if ruin
206 Leaped from his eyes. So looks the chafèd lion
207 Upon the daring huntsman that has galled him,
208 Then makes him nothing. I must read this paper;
I fear, the story of his anger. 'Tis so.
210 This paper has undone me. 'Tis th' account
Of all that world of wealth I have drawn together
For mine own ends – indeed to gain the popedom
And fee my friends in Rome. O negligence
214 Fit for a fool to fall by! What cross devil
215 Made me put this main secret in the packet
I sent the king? Is there no way to cure this?
No new device to beat this from his brains?
I know 'twill stir him strongly; yet I know

---

192 *have* have been   197 *chiding* i.e., noisily turbulent   198 *break* withstand (as in "breakwater")   206 *chafèd* enraged   207 *galled* wounded   208 *makes . . . nothing* annihilates him   214 *cross* thwarting   215 *main* principal, vitally important

A way, if it take right, in spite of fortune,   219
Will bring me off again. What's this? "To th' pope"?   220
The letter (as I live) with all the business
I writ to's holiness. Nay then, farewell!
I have touched the highest point of all my greatness,
And from that full meridian of my glory   224
I haste now to my setting. I shall fall
Like a bright exhalation in the evening,   226
And no man see me more.
   Enter to Wolsey the Dukes of Norfolk and Suffolk, the
   Earl of Surrey, and the Lord Chamberlain.
NORFOLK
Hear the king's pleasure, cardinal, who commands you
To render up the great seal presently   229
Into our hands and to confine yourself   230
To Asher House, my Lord of Winchester's,
Till you hear further from his highness.
WOLSEY   Stay!
Where's your commission, lords? Words cannot carry   233
Authority so weighty.   234
SUFFOLK   Who dare cross 'em,
Bearing the king's will from his mouth expressly?
WOLSEY
Till I find more than will or words to do it   236
(I mean your malice) know, officious lords,
I dare and must deny it. Now I feel
Of what coarse metal ye are molded, envy,   239
How eagerly ye follow my disgraces   240
As if it fed ye, and how sleek and wanton   241
Ye appear in everything may bring my ruin!
Follow your envious courses, men of malice.
You have Christian warrant for 'em, and no doubt   244

---

219 *take right* succeed   220 *bring me off* rescue me, exonerate me   224 *full
meridian* apogee   226 *exhalation* meteor (metaphoric allusion to the fall of
Lucifer)   229 *presently* immediately   233 *commission* written authority
234 *cross* oppose   236 *do it* i.e., relinquish my authority   239 *envy* malice
241 *wanton* headlong, shamefully eager   244 *Christian warrant* (ironic)

245   In time will find their fit rewards. That seal
       You ask with such a violence, the king
       (Mine and your master) with his own hand gave me,
248   Bade me enjoy it, with the place and honors,
       During my life, and to confirm his goodness
250   Ties it by letters patents. Now who'll take it?
       SURREY
       The king that gave it.
       WOLSEY   It must be himself then.
       SURREY
       Thou art a proud traitor, priest.
       WOLSEY   Proud lord, thou liest!
253   Within these forty hours Surrey durst better
       Have burnt that tongue than said so.
       SURREY   Thy ambition
255   (Thou scarlet sin) robbed this bewailing land
       Of noble Buckingham, my father-in-law.
       The heads of all thy brother cardinals
258   (With thee and all thy best parts bound together)
259   Weighed not a hair of his. Plague of your policy!
260   You sent me Deputy for Ireland,
       Far from his succor, from the king, from all
262   That might have mercy on the fault thou gav'st him,
       Whilst your great goodness, out of holy pity,
       Absolved him with an ax.
       WOLSEY   This, and all else
265   This talking lord can lay upon my credit,
       I answer is most false. The duke by law
       Found his deserts. How innocent I was
268   From any private malice in his end,
       His noble jury and foul cause can witness.
270   If I loved many words, lord, I should tell you

---

245 *find* meet with   248 *place* position (of Lord Chancellor)   250 *letters patents* open (public) documents   253 *forty hours* (a round number)   255 *scarlet* (alluding both to the robes of a cardinal and the heinousness of the sin)   258 *parts* qualities   259 *policy* conniving   262 *fault* offense; *gav'st him* accused him of   265 *credit* good name   268 *From* of

You have as little honesty as honor,
That in the way of loyalty and truth   272
Toward the king, my ever royal master,
Dare mate a sounder man than Surrey can be   274
And all that love his follies.
SURREY   By my soul,
Your long coat, priest, protects you; thou shouldst feel
My sword i' th' lifeblood of thee else. My lords,
Can ye endure to hear this arrogance?
And from this fellow? If we live thus tamely,   279
To be thus jaded by a piece of scarlet,   280
Farewell nobility: let his grace go forward
And dare us with his cap, like larks.   282
WOLSEY   All goodness
Is poison to thy stomach.
SURREY   Yes, that goodness
Of gleaning all the land's wealth into one,
Into your own hands, cardinal, by extortion;
The goodness of your intercepted packets
You writ to th' pope against the king. Your goodness,
Since you provoke me, shall be most notorious.   288
My Lord of Norfolk, as you are truly noble,   .
As you respect the common good, the state   290
Of our despised nobility, our issues   291
(Whom, if he live, will scarce be gentlemen),
Produce the grand sum of his sins, the articles   293
Collected from his life. I'll startle you
Worse than the sacring bell when the brown wench   295
Lay kissing in your arms, lord cardinal.

---

272 *That* I that   274 *mate* match   279 *tamely* meekly   280 *jaded* cowed,
humiliated   282 *dare* dazzle (alludes to a method of catching larks with the
help of a mirror and red cloth)   288 *notorious* openly known   291 *issues*
male heirs   293 *articles* counts of indictment   295 *sacring bell* bell sum-
moning to prayers; *brown wench* (implying a sunburned slut from the lower
classes, gentry women supposedly being characterized by their fair, protected
skins)

WOLSEY
How much, methinks, I could despise this man
But that I am bound in charity against it.
NORFOLK
Those articles, my lord, are in the king's hand.
300   But thus much — they are foul ones.
WOLSEY   So much fairer
And spotless shall mine innocence arise
When the king knows my truth.
SURREY   This cannot save you.
I thank my memory, I yet remember
Some of these articles, and out they shall!
Now if you can blush and cry guilty, cardinal,
You'll show a little honesty.
WOLSEY   Speak on, sir,
307   I dare your worst objections. If I blush,
It is to see a nobleman want manners.
SURREY
309   I had rather want those than my head. Have at you!
310   First, that without the king's assent or knowledge
311   You wrought to be a legate, by which power
You maimed the jurisdiction of all bishops.
NORFOLK
Then, that all you writ to Rome, or else
314   To foreign princes, *"Ego et Rex meus"*
315   Was still inscribed, in which you brought the king
To be your servant.
SUFFOLK   Then, that without the knowledge
Either of king or council, when you went
318   Ambassador to the emperor, you made bold
To carry into Flanders the great seal.

---

300 *thus much* i.e., I can tell you this much   307 *objections* accusations
309 *Have at you* (phrase of challenge or imminent attack)   311 *wrought*
contrived; *legate* pope's official representative   314 *Ego . . . meus* I and my
king   315 *still* always   318 *emperor* i.e., Charles V

SURREY
  Item, you sent a large commission   *320*
  To Gregory de Cassado to conclude,
  Without the king's will or the state's allowance,   *322*
  A league between his highness and Ferrara.
SUFFOLK
  That out of mere ambition you have caused   *324*
  Your holy hat to be stamped on the king's coin.   *325*
SURREY
  Then, that you have sent innumerable substance   *326*
  (By what means got, I leave to your own conscience)
  To furnish Rome and to prepare the ways   *328*
  You have for dignities, to the mere undoing   *329*
  Of all the kingdom. Many more there are,   *330*
  Which, since they are of you, and odious,
  I will not taint my mouth with.
CHAMBERLAIN   O my lord,
  Press not a falling man too far! 'Tis virtue.
  His faults lie open to the laws; let them,
  Not you, correct him. My heart weeps to see him
  So little of his great self.
SURREY   I forgive him.
SUFFOLK
  Lord cardinal, the king's further pleasure is —
  Because all those things you have done of late
  By your power legative within this kingdom   *339*
  Fall into th' compass of a praemunire —   *340*
  That therefore such a writ be sued against you,   *341*
  To forfeit all your goods, lands, tenements,

---

322 *allowance* permission   324 *mere* sheer   325 *Your . . . coin* (Wolsey had illegitimately caused his image to be imprinted on the coins known as groats) 326 *innumerable substance* countless wealth   328 *furnish* supply   329 *dignities* honors; *mere undoing* utter ruin   339 *legative* as legate   340 *compass* scope; *praemunire* writ by which a person was charged with asserting papal jurisdiction in England, thus preempting royal authority   341 *sued* applied for

Chattels, and whatsoever, and to be
344 Out of the king's protection. This is my charge.
NORFOLK
And so we'll leave you to your meditations ·
How to live better. For your stubborn answer
About the giving back the great seal to us,
The king shall know it, and (no doubt) shall thank you.
349 So fare you well, my little good lord cardinal.
                                         Exeunt all but Wolsey.

WOLSEY
350 So farewell to the little good you bear me.
Farewell? A long farewell to all my greatness!
This is the state of man: today he puts forth
The tender leaves of hopes; tomorrow blossoms
354 And bears his blushing honors thick upon him;
The third day comes a frost, a killing frost,
356 And when he thinks, good easy man, full surely
His greatness is a-ripening, nips his root,
And then he falls as I do. I have ventured,
359 Like little wanton boys that swim on bladders,
360 This many summers in a sea of glory,
But far beyond my depth. My high-blown pride
At length broke under me, and now has left me,
Weary and old with service, to the mercy
364 Of a rude stream that must for ever hide me.
Vain pomp and glory of this world, I hate ye!
I feel my heart new opened. O, how wretched
Is that poor man that hangs on princes' favors!
There is betwixt that smile we would aspire to,
369 That sweet aspect of princes, and their ruin,
370 More pangs and fears than wars or women have;
And when he falls, he falls like Lucifer,

---

344 *Out . . . protection* i.e., without legal protection   **349** *little good* (playing on the conventional salutation "my good lord")   **354** *blushing* glowing **356** *easy* comfortable, easygoing   **359** *wanton* reckless   **364** *rude* rough **369** *their ruin* the ruin they cause

Never to hope again.
    Enter Cromwell, standing amazed.
                        Why how now, Cromwell?
CROMWELL
  I have no power to speak, sir.
WOLSEY   What, amazed
  At my misfortunes? Can thy spirit wonder
  A great man should decline? Nay, an you weep,   375
  I am fall'n indeed.
CROMWELL   How does your grace?
WOLSEY   Why well;
  Never so truly happy, my good Cromwell.
  I know myself now, and I feel within me
  A peace above all earthly dignities,
  A still and quiet conscience. The king has cured me –   380
  I humbly thank his grace – and from these shoulders,
  These ruined pillars, out of pity taken
  A load would sink a navy, too much honor.
  O 'tis a burden, Cromwell, 'tis a burden
  Too heavy for a man that hopes for heaven.
CROMWELL
  I am glad your grace has made that right use of it.
WOLSEY
  I hope I have. I am able now, methinks,
  Out of a fortitude of soul I feel,
  To endure more miseries and greater far
  Than my weakhearted enemies dare offer.   390
  What news abroad?
CROMWELL   The heaviest and the worst
  Is your displeasure with the king.   392
WOLSEY   God bless him!
CROMWELL
  The next is that Sir Thomas More is chosen
  Lord Chancellor in your place.
WOLSEY   That's somewhat sudden.

---

375 *an* if   392 *your . . . king* i.e., the king's displeasure with you

But he's a learnèd man. May he continue
Long in his highness' favor, and do justice
For truth's sake and his conscience; that his bones,
When he has run his course and sleeps in blessings,
399   May have a tomb of orphans' tears wept on him.
400   What more?

CROMWELL   That Cranmer is returned with welcome;
Installed Lord Archbishop of Canterbury.

WOLSEY
That's news indeed.

CROMWELL   Last, that the Lady Anne,
·Whom the king hath in secrecy long married,
This day was viewed in open as his queen,
405   Going to chapel; and the voice is now
Only about her coronation.

WOLSEY
There was the weight that pulled me down. O
   Cromwell,
408   The king has gone beyond me. All my glories
In that one woman I have lost for ever.
410   No sun shall ever usher forth mine honors
411   Or gild again the noble troops that waited
Upon my smiles. Go get thee from me, Cromwell!
I am a poor fall'n man, unworthy now
To be thy lord and master. Seek the king
(That sun, I pray, may never set). I have told him
What and how true thou art. He will advance thee.
Some little memory of me will stir him
(I know his noble nature) not to let
Thy hopeful service perish too. Good Cromwell,
420   Neglect him not; make use now, and provide
For thine own future safety.

CROMWELL   O my lord,

---

399 *a tomb . . . him* (the Lord Chancellor was legal guardian of orphaned children)   **405** *voice* general talk   **408** *gone beyond* outstripped, overreached   **411** *troops* retainers   **420** *make use* take advantage

Must I then leave you? Must I needs forgo
So good, so noble, and so true a master?
Bear witness, all that have not hearts of iron,
With what a sorrow Cromwell leaves his lord.
The king shall have my service, but my pray'rs
For ever and for ever shall be yours.
WOLSEY
Cromwell, I did not think to shed a tear
In all my miseries, but thou hast forced me
(Out of thy honest truth) to play the woman.   430
Let's dry our eyes, and thus far hear me, Cromwell,
And when I am forgotten, as I shall be,
And sleep in dull cold marble, where no mention
Of me more must be heard of, say I taught thee.
Say Wolsey, that once trod the ways of glory
And sounded all the depths and shoals of honor,   436
Found thee a way (out of his wrack) to rise in,   437
A sure and safe one, though thy master missed it.
Mark but my fall and that that ruined me.
Cromwell, I charge thee, fling away ambition!   440
By that sin fell the angels; how can man then
(The image of his Maker) hope to win by it?   442
Love thyself last, cherish those hearts that hate thee;
Corruption wins not more than honesty.
Still in thy right hand carry gentle peace   445
To silence envious tongues. Be just, and fear not.
Let all the ends thou aim'st at be thy country's,
Thy God's, and truth's. Then if thou fall'st, O Cromwell,
Thou fall'st a blessed martyr.
Serve the king. And prithee lead me in,   450
There take an inventory of all I have
To the last penny: 'tis the king's. My robe
And my integrity to heaven is all

---

430 *truth* loyalty 436 *shoals* shallows 437 *wrack* shipwreck 442 *win*
profit 445 *Still* constantly

I dare now call mine own. O Cromwell, Cromwell,
Had I but served my God with half the zeal
I served my king, he would not in mine age
457   Have left me naked to mine enemies.
CROMWELL
   Good sir, have patience.
WOLSEY   So I have. Farewell
   The hopes of court; my hopes in heaven do dwell.
                               Exeunt.

                         *

   ∾ **IV.1**   *Enter two Gentlemen, meeting one another.*

FIRST GENTLEMAN
   You're well met once again.
SECOND GENTLEMAN   So are you.
FIRST GENTLEMAN
   You come to take your stand here, and behold
   The Lady Anne pass from her coronation?
SECOND GENTLEMAN
   'Tis all my business. At our last encounter
   The Duke of Buckingham came from his trial.
FIRST GENTLEMAN
   'Tis very true, but that time offered sorrow,
   This, general joy.
SECOND GENTLEMAN
                   'Tis well. The citizens
8   I am sure have shown at full their royal minds –
9   As let 'em have their rights, they are ever forward –
10   In celebration of this day with shows,
   Pageants, and sights of honor.

---

457 *naked* defenseless
   IV.1 A street in Westminster   8 *royal minds* devotion to royalty   9 *As let . . . rights* to give them their due

FIRST GENTLEMAN   Never greater,
  Nor, I'll assure you, better taken, sir.   12
SECOND GENTLEMAN
  May I be bold to ask what that contains,
  That paper in your hand?
FIRST GENTLEMAN   Yes, 'tis the list
  Of those that claim their offices this day,
  By custom of the coronation.
  The Duke of Suffolk is the first, and claims
  To be high steward; next, the Duke of Norfolk,
  He to be earl marshal. You may read the rest.
SECOND GENTLEMAN
  I thank you, sir. Had I not known those customs,   20
  I should have been beholding to your paper.   21
  But, I beseech you, what's become of Katherine,
  The princess dowager? How goes her business?
FIRST GENTLEMAN
  That I can tell you too. The Archbishop
  Of Canterbury, accompanied with other
  Learnèd and reverend fathers of his order,
  Held a late court at Dunstable, six miles off   27
  From Ampthill, where the princess lay, to which   28
  She was often cited by them, but appeared not;   29
  And to be short, for not-appearance and   30
  The king's late scruple, by the main assent   31
  Of all these learned men she was divorced
  And the late marriage made of none effect,   33
  Since which she was removed to Kimbolton,
  Where she remains now sick.
SECOND GENTLEMAN   Alas good lady.
    [Trumpets.]

---

12 *taken* appreciated   21 *beholding* indebted   27 *late* recent   28 *lay* resided
29 *cited* summoned   31 *late* former; *main assent* consensus   33 *made of
none effect* annulled

36   The trumpets sound. Stand close, the queen is coming.
Hautboys.

The Order of the Coronation

1. *A lively flourish of trumpets.*
2. *Then two Judges.*
3. *Lord Chancellor, with purse and mace before him.*
4. *Choristers singing. Music.*
5. *Mayor of London, bearing the mace. Then Garter, in his coat of arms, and on his head he wore a gilt copper crown.*
6. *Marquis Dorset, bearing a scepter of gold, on his head a demicoronal of gold. With him the Earl of Surrey, bearing the rod of silver with the dove, crowned with an earl's coronet. Collars of Esses.*
7. *Duke of Suffolk, in his robe of estate, his coronet on his head, bearing a long white wand, as high steward. With him the Duke of Norfolk, with the rod of marshalship, a coronet on his head. Collars of Esses.*
8. *A canopy borne by four of the Cinque Ports; under it the Queen in her robe; in her hair, richly adorned with pearl, crowned. On each side her the Bishops of London and Winchester.*
9. *The old Duchess of Norfolk, in a coronal of gold, wrought with flowers, bearing the Queen's train.*
10. *Certain Ladies or Countesses, with plain circlets of gold without flowers.*

        Exeunt, first passing over the stage in order and state, and then a great flourish of trumpets.

---

36 s.d. *Hautboys* early form of oboe; **item 3** *Lord Chancellor* (now Sir Thomas More); **item 5** *Garter* the chief herald, known as the Garter King-of-Arms; **item 6** *demicoronal* small, crownlike circlet; **items 6, 7** *Collars of Esses* ornamental chains made with linked letters "S"; **item 7** *estate* state; **item 8** *Cinque Ports* barons of the five Channel ports of Hastings, Sandwich, Dover, Romney, and Hythe; *in her hair* with her hair hanging loose (customary for brides)

SECOND GENTLEMAN
   A royal train, believe me. These I know.   37
   Who's that that bears the scepter?
FIRST GENTLEMAN   Marquis Dorset,
   And that the Earl of Surrey with the rod.
SECOND GENTLEMAN
   A bold brave gentleman. That should be   40
   The Duke of Suffolk.
FIRST GENTLEMAN   'Tis the same: high steward.
SECOND GENTLEMAN
   And that my Lord of Norfolk?
FIRST GENTLEMAN   Yes.
SECOND GENTLEMAN *[Looks on the Queen.]* Heaven bless
     thee,
   Thou hast the sweetest face I ever looked on.
   Sir, as I have a soul, she is an angel;
   Our king has all the Indies in his arms,   45
   And more, and richer, when he strains that lady.   46
   I cannot blame his conscience.
FIRST GENTLEMAN   They that bear
   The cloth of honor over her are four barons   48
   Of the Cinque Ports.
SECOND GENTLEMAN
   Those men are happy, and so are all are near her.   50
   I take it, she that carries up the train   51
   Is that old noble lady, Duchess of Norfolk.
FIRST GENTLEMAN
   It is, and all the rest are countesses.
SECOND GENTLEMAN
   Their coronets say so. These are stars indeed –   54
FIRST GENTLEMAN
   And sometimes falling ones.   55

---

37 *train* retinue   45 *Indies* i.e., limitless riches (both the East and West Indies were regarded as sources of wealth)   46 *strains* embraces, makes love to
48 *cloth of honor* canopy   50 *all* all who   51 *carries . . . train* bears Anne's
long robe   54 *stars* (term for the nobility)   55 *falling* (with sexual innuendo)

SECOND GENTLEMAN   No more of that.
                                    [Exit procession.]
        Enter a third Gentleman.
FIRST GENTLEMAN
    God save you, sir. Where have you been broiling?
THIRD GENTLEMAN
57 Among the crowd i' th' Abbey, where a finger
    Could not be wedged in more. I am stifled
59 With the mere rankness of their joy.
SECOND GENTLEMAN   You saw
60 The ceremony?
THIRD GENTLEMAN   That I did.
FIRST GENTLEMAN   How was it?
THIRD GENTLEMAN
61 Well worth the seeing.
SECOND GENTLEMAN   Good sir, speak it to us.
THIRD GENTLEMAN
    As well as I am able. The rich stream
    Of lords and ladies, having brought the queen
64 To a prepared place in the choir, fell off
    A distance from her, while her grace sat down
    To rest awhile, some half an hour or so,
67 In a rich chair of state, opposing freely
    The beauty of her person to the people.
69 Believe me, sir, she is the goodliest woman
70 That ever lay by man; which when the people
    Had the full view of, such a noise arose
72 As the shrouds make at sea in a stiff tempest,
    As loud, and to as many tunes. Hats, cloaks
74 (Doublets, I think) flew up; and had their faces
    Been loose, this day they had been lost. Such joy
    I never saw before. Great-bellied women

---

57 *th' Abbey* Westminster Abbey (scene of the coronation)   59 *mere rankness*
sheer exuberance (with possible allusion to the smell of the crowd)   61 *speak*
describe   64 *fell off* withdrew   67 *opposing* exposing   69 *goodliest* best-look-
ing   72 *shrouds* sail ropes   74 *Doublets* close-fitting body garments worn by
men

That had not half a week to go, like rams   77
In the old time of war, would shake the press   78
And make 'em reel before 'em. No man living
Could say "This is my wife" there, all were woven   80
So strangely in one piece.   81
SECOND GENTLEMAN   But what followed?
THIRD GENTLEMAN
    At length her grace rose and with modest paces   82
    Came to the altar, where she kneeled, and saintlike
    Cast her fair eyes to heaven and prayed devoutly,
    Then rose again and bowed her to the people,
    When by the Archbishop of Canterbury
    She had all the royal makings of a queen,   87
    As holy oil, Edward Confessor's crown,   88
    The rod, and bird of peace, and all such emblems
    Laid nobly on her; which performed, the choir   90
    With all the choicest music of the kingdom   91
    Together sung "Te Deum." So she parted,   92
    And with the same full state packed back again   93
    To York Place, where the feast is held.
FIRST GENTLEMAN   Sir,
    You must no more call it York Place. That's past,
    For since the cardinal fell that title's lost;
    'Tis now the king's, and called Whitehall.
THIRD GENTLEMAN   I know it,
    But 'tis so lately altered that the old name
    Is fresh about me.
SECOND GENTLEMAN What two reverend bishops
    Were those that went on each side of the queen?   100
THIRD GENTLEMAN
    Stokely and Gardiner, the one of Winchester,
    Newly preferred from the king's secretary,   102

---

77 *rams* battering-rams   78 *shake the press* jostle the crowd   81 *piece* (of fabric)   82 *modest* moderate   87 *makings* accoutrements   88 *As* namely   91 *music* musicians   92 *Te Deum* thee, God (we praise); *parted* departed   93 *state* pomp; *packed* proceeded   102 *preferred* advanced

The other, London.

SECOND GENTLEMAN He of Winchester
Is held no great good lover of the archbishop's,
The virtuous Cranmer.

THIRD GENTLEMAN   All the land knows that.
However, yet there is no great breach. When it comes,
Cranmer will find a friend will not shrink from him.

SECOND GENTLEMAN
Who may that be, I pray you?

THIRD GENTLEMAN   Thomas Cromwell,
A man in much esteem with th' king, and truly
110   A worthy friend. The king has made him
111   Master o' th' Jewel House,
And one, already, of the Privy Council.

SECOND GENTLEMAN
He will deserve more.

THIRD GENTLEMAN   Yes, without all doubt.
Come, gentlemen, ye shall go my way,
Which is to th' court, and there ye shall be my guests.
116   Something I can command. As I walk thither,
I'll tell ye more.

BOTH   You may command us, sir.   *Exeunt.*

*

   *IV.2 Enter Katherine Dowager, sick, led between
Griffith, her gentleman usher, and Patience, her
woman.*

GRIFFITH
How does your grace?

KATHERINE   O Griffith, sick to death.
My legs like loaden branches bow to th' earth,
Willing to leave their burden. Reach a chair.

---

111 *Master o' th' Jewel House* keeper of the crown jewels, royal treasure, etc.
116 *Something . . . command* i.e., I can scratch up something to eat
   IV.2 Katherine's apartments (at Kimbolton)

So now, methinks, I feel a little ease.
Didst thou not tell me, Griffith, as thou led'st me,
That the great child of honor, Cardinal Wolsey,   6
Was dead?
GRIFFITH   Yes, madam, but I think your grace,
  Out of the pain you suffered, gave no ear to't.
KATHERINE
  Prithee, good Griffith, tell me how he died.
  If well, he stepped before me happily   10
  For my example.   11
GRIFFITH   Well, the voice goes, madam,
  For after the stout Earl Northumberland   12
  Arrested him at York and brought him forward
  As a man sorely tainted, to his answer,   14
  He fell sick suddenly, and grew so ill
  He could not sit his mule.
KATHERINE   Alas, poor man.
GRIFFITH
  At last, with easy roads, he came to Leicester,   17
  Lodged in the abbey, where the reverend abbot
  With all his covent honorably received him,   19
  To whom he gave these words: "O father abbot,   20
  An old man, broken with the storms of state,
  Is come to lay his weary bones among ye.
  Give him a little earth for charity!"
  So went to bed, where eagerly his sickness
  Pursued him still, and three nights after this,
  After the hour of eight, which he himself
  Foretold should be his last, full of repentance,
  Continual meditations, tears and sorrows,   28
  He gave his honors to the world again,
  His blessèd part to heaven, and slept in peace.   30

---

6 *child of honor* (normally refers to one of noble birth; here ironic?)   10 *happily* (1) perhaps, (2) fortunately   11 *voice* common talk   12 *stout* (1) strong, (2) haughty   14 *sorely tainted* severely discredited   17 *roads* stages of a journey   19 *covent* convent   28 *sorrows* expressions of sorrow   30 *blessèd part* i.e., soul

KATHERINE
  So may he rest, his faults lie gently on him!
32 Yet thus far, Griffith, give me leave to speak him,
  And yet with charity. He was a man
34 Of an unbounded stomach, ever ranking
35 Himself with princes; one that by suggestion
36 Tied all the kingdom. Simony was fair play;
37 His own opinion was his law. I' th' presence
38 He would say untruths, and be ever double
  Both in his words and meaning. He was never
40 (But where he meant to ruin) pitiful.
  His promises were, as he then was, mighty;
  But his performance, as he is now, nothing.
43 Of his own body he was ill, and gave
  The clergy ill example.
GRIFFITH   Noble madam,
  Men's evil manners live in brass; their virtues
  We write in water. May it please your highness
  To hear me speak his good now?
KATHERINE   Yes, good Griffith,
  I were malicious else.
GRIFFITH   This cardinal,
  Though from an humble stock, undoubtedly
50 Was fashioned to much honor. From his cradle
51 He was a scholar, and a ripe and good one,
  Exceeding wise, fair-spoken, and persuading;
53 Lofty and sour to them that loved him not,
  But to those men that sought him, sweet as summer.
  And though he were unsatisfied in getting
  (Which was a sin), yet in bestowing, madam,
  He was most princely. Ever witness for him
58 Those twins of learning that he raised in you,

---

32 *speak* describe   34 *unbounded stomach* limitless ambition   35 *suggestion* double-dealing   36 *Tied* fettered; *Simony* trafficking in church preferments   37 *presence* royal presence chamber   38 *double* deceitful   40 *pitiful* compassionate   43 *ill* corrupt   50 *fashioned to* cut out for   51 *ripe* accomplished   53 *Lofty* haughty   58 *twins of learning* i.e., colleges; *raised* founded

Ipswich and Oxford; one of which fell with him,
Unwilling to outlive the good that did it;   60
The other, though unfinished, yet so famous,
So excellent in art, and still so rising,   62
That Christendom shall ever speak his virtue.
His overthrow heaped happiness upon him,
For then, and not till then, he felt himself,   65
And found the blessedness of being little.
And, to add greater honors to his age
Than man could give him, he died fearing God.
KATHERINE
After my death I wish no other herald,
No other speaker of my living actions   70
To keep mine honor from corruption,
But such an honest chronicler as Griffith.
Whom I most hated living, thou hast made me,
With thy religious truth and modesty,   74
Now, in his ashes, honor. Peace be with him!
Patience, be near me still, and set me lower;
I have not long to trouble thee. Good Griffith,
Cause the musicians play me that sad note   78
I named my knell, whilst I sit meditating
On that celestial harmony I go to.   80
    Sad and solemn music.
GRIFFITH
She is asleep. Good wench, let's sit down quiet
For fear we wake her. Softly, gentle Patience.   82

The Vision
*Enter, solemnly tripping one after another, six personages
clad in white robes, wearing on their heads garlands of
bays, and golden vizards on their faces, branches of bays
or palm in their hands. They first congee unto her, then*

---

60 *good* good man; *did* created   **62** *rising* (both as a building and an influ-
ence)   **65** *felt himself* knew himself   **70** *living* while alive   **74** *modesty* moderation   **78** *note* melody   **82 s.d.** *bays* laurel; *vizards* masks; *congee* bow

*dance; and, at certain changes, the first two hold a spare
garland over her head; at which the other four make
reverent curtsies. Then the two that held the garland
deliver the same to the other next two, who observe the
same order in their changes, and holding the garland
over her head; which done, they deliver the same
garland to tshe last two, who likewise observe the same
order; at which (as it were by inspiration) she makes (in
her sleep) signs of rejoicing and holdeth up her hands to
heaven. And so in their dancing vanish, carrying the
garland with them. The music continues.*

KATHERINE
  Spirit of peace, where are ye? Are ye all gone
  And leave me here in wretchedness behind ye?
GRIFFITH
  Madam, we are here.
KATHERINE   It is not you I call for.
  Saw ye none enter since I slept?
GRIFFITH   None, madam.
KATHERINE
  No? Saw you not even now a blessed troop
  Invite me to a banquet, whose bright faces
  Cast thousand beams upon me like the sun?
90 They promised me eternal happiness
  And brought me garlands, Griffith, which I feel
  I am not worthy yet to wear; I shall assuredly.
GRIFFITH
  I am most joyful, madam, such good dreams
94 · Possess your fancy.
KATHERINE   Bid the music leave.
95 They are harsh and heavy to me.
      Music ceases.
PATIENCE   Do you note

---

82 s.d. (cont'd) *changes* figures in the dance   **94** *Possess* occupy; *music* musicians; *leave* cease playing   **95** *heavy* oppressive

How much her grace is altered on the sudden?
How long her face is drawn? How pale she looks,
And of an earthly cold? Mark her eyes!   98
GRIFFITH
She is going, wench. Pray, pray!
PATIENCE   Heaven comfort her!
    Enter a Messenger.
MESSENGER
An't like your grace –   100
KATHERINE   You are a saucy fellow!
    Deserve we no more reverence?
GRIFFITH   You are to blame,
Knowing she will not lose her wonted greatness,   102
To use so rude behavior. Go to, kneel!
MESSENGER
I humbly do entreat your highness' pardon;
My haste made me unmannerly. There is staying   105
A gentleman sent from the king, to see you.
KATHERINE
Admit him entrance, Griffith. But this fellow   107
Let me ne'er see again.   *[Exit Messenger].*
    Enter Lord Capuchius.
                            If my sight fail not,
You should be lord ambassador from the emperor,
My royal nephew, and your name Capuchius.   110
CAPUCHIUS
Madam, the same. Your servant.
KATHERINE   O my lord,
The times and titles now are altered strangely
With me since first you knew me. But I pray you,
What is your pleasure with me?
CAPUCHIUS   Noble lady,
First mine own service to your grace. The next,
The king's request that I would visit you,

---

98 *cold* coldness (taken as a sign of impending death) 102 *lose* forgo;
wonted accustomed   105 *staying* waiting   107 *Admit* allow

Who grieves much for your weakness, and by me
118 Sends you his princely commendations,
And heartily entreats you take good comfort.
KATHERINE
120 O my good lord, that comfort comes too late,
'Tis like a pardon after execution.
122 That gentle physic, given in time, had cured me,
But now I am past all comforts here but prayers.
How does his highness?
CAPUCHIUS   Madam, in good health.
KATHERINE
So may he ever do, and ever flourish,
When I shall dwell with worms, and my poor name
Banished the kingdom. Patience, is that letter
– I caused you write yet sent away?
PATIENCE   No, madam.
   [Gives it to Katherine.]
KATHERINE
Sir, I most humbly pray you to deliver
130 This to my lord the king.
CAPUCHIUS   Most willing, madam.
KATHERINE
In which I have commended to his goodness
132 The model of our chaste loves, his young daughter –
The dews of heaven fall thick in blessings on her! –
134 Beseeching him to give her virtuous breeding –
She is young and of a noble modest nature;
I hope she will deserve well – and a little
137 To love her for her mother's sake, that loved him,
Heaven knows how dearly. My next poor petition
Is that his noble grace would have some pity
140 Upon my wretched women, that so long
141 Have followed both my fortunes faithfully, .
Of which there is not one, I dare avow

---

118 *commendations* compliments   122 *had* would have   132 *model* image,
token; *our* i.e., hers and Henry's   134 *virtuous breeding* good upbringing
and education   137 *him* i.e., Henry   141 *both* i.e., good and bad

(And now I should not lie), but will deserve
For virtue and true beauty of the soul,
For honesty and decent carriage,   145
A right good husband – let him be a noble –
And sure those men are happy that shall have 'em.
The last is for my men – they are the poorest
But poverty could never draw 'em from me –
That they may have their wages duly paid 'em,   *150*
And something over to remember me by.
If heaven had pleased to have given me longer life
And able means, we had not parted thus.   153
These are the whole contents. And, good my lord,
By that you love the dearest in this world,
As you wish Christian peace to souls departed,
Stand these poor people's friend, and urge the king   157
To do me this last right.
CAPUCHIUS   By heaven I will,
Or let me lose the fashion of a man!   159
KATHERINE
I thank you, honest lord. Remember me   *160*
In all humility unto his highness.
Say his long trouble now is passing
Out of this world. Tell him in death I blessed him,
For so I will. Mine eyes grow dim. Farewell,
My lord. Griffith, farewell. Nay, Patience,
You must not leave me yet. I must to bed;
Call in more women. When I am dead, good wench,
Let me be used with honor. Strew me over
With maiden flowers, that all the world may know   169
I was a chaste wife to my grave. Embalm me,   *170*
Then lay me forth. Although unqueened, yet like   171
A queen, and daughter to a king, inter me.
I can no more.   *Exeunt, leading Katherine.*

---

145 *decent carriage* proper demeanor   153 *able* sufficient   157 *Stand* remain   159 *fashion* nature, character   169 *maiden flowers* (emblems of
chastity)   171 *lay me forth* lay me out

*

∾ **V.1** *Enter Gardiner, Bishop of Winchester, a Page*
with a torch before him, met by Sir Thomas Lovell.

GARDINER
  It's one o'clock, boy, is't not?
BOY   It hath struck.
GARDINER
  These should be hours for necessities,
3   Not for delights; times to repair our nature
  With comforting repose, and not for us
  To waste these times. Good hour of night, Sir Thomas:
  Whither so late?
LOVELL   Came you from the king, my lord?
GARDINER
7   I did, Sir Thomas, and left him at primero
  With the Duke of Suffolk.
LOVELL   I must to him too
  Before he go to bed. I'll take my leave.
GARDINER
10   Not yet, Sir Thomas Lovell. What's the matter?
11   It seems you are in haste. An if there be
  No great offense belongs to't, give your friend
13   Some touch of your late business. Affairs that walk
  (As they say spirits do) at midnight have
  In them a wilder nature than the business
  That seeks dispatch by day.
LOVELL   My lord, I love you,
17   And durst commend a secret to your ear
  Much weightier than this work. The queen's in labor,
19   They say in great extremity, and feared

V.1 The royal palace **3** *repair* restore **7** *primero* a gambling card game **11**
An if if truly **13** *touch* hint; *walk* continue **17** *commend* entrust **19**
feared i.e., it is feared that

She'll with the labor end.   20
GARDINER   The fruit she goes with
I pray for heartily, that it may find
Good time, and live. But for the stock, Sir Thomas,   22
I wish it grubbed up now.   23
LOVELL   Methinks I could
Cry the amen, and yet my conscience says   24
She's a good creature and sweet lady, does
Deserve our better wishes.
GARDINER   But, sir, sir,
Hear me, Sir Thomas! You're a gentleman
Of mine own way. I know you wise, religious,   28
And let me tell you it will ne'er be well –
'Twill not, Sir Thomas Lovell, take't of me –   30
Till Cranmer, Cromwell, her two hands, and she
Sleep in their graves.
LOVELL   Now, sir, you speak of two
The most remarked i' th' kingdom. As for Cromwell,   33
Beside that of the Jewel House, is made Master   34
O' th' Rolls and the king's secretary; further, sir,
Stands in the gap and trade of more preferments,   36
With which the time will load him. Th' archbishop   37
Is the king's hand and tongue, and who dare speak
One syllable against him?
GARDINER   Yes, yes, Sir Thomas,
There are that dare, and I myself have ventured   40
To speak my mind of him; and indeed this day,
Sir (I may tell it you), I think I have
Incensed the lords o' th' council that he is   43
(For so I know he is, they know he is)
A most arch-heretic, a pestilence   45

20 *fruit she goes with* i.e., the child she bears   22 *Good time* good fortune; *the stock,* i.e., the parent   23 *grubbed up* rooted out   24 *Cry the amen* assent   28 *Of mine own way* i.e., of my own Catholic persuasion   33 *remarked* noted, prominent   34–35 *Master . . . Rolls* judge of the court of appeal   36 *gap and trade* opening and beaten path; *more preferments* additional high offices and honors   37 *the time* the unfolding course of events   43 *Incensed* stirred up and convinced   45 *pestilence* plague

46   That does infect the land; with which they moved
47   Have broken with the king, who hath so far
      Given ear to our complaint – of his great grace
49   And princely care, foreseeing those fell mischiefs
50   Our reasons laid before him – hath commanded
      Tomorrow morning to the council board
52   He be convented. He's a rank weed, Sir Thomas,
      And we must root him out. From your affairs
      I hinder you too long. Good night, Sir Thomas.
LOVELL
55   Many good nights, my lord. I rest your servant.
                              Exeunt Gardiner and Page.
          Enter King and Suffolk.
KING
      Charles, I will play no more tonight,
      My mind's not on't, you are too hard for me.
SUFFOLK
      Sir, I did never win of you before.
KING
      But little, Charles,
60   Nor shall not when my fancy's on my play.
      Now, Lovell, from the queen what is the news?
LOVELL
62   I could not personally deliver to her
      What you commanded me, but by her woman
      I sent your message, who returned her thanks
      In the great'st humbleness, and desired your highness
      Most heartily to pray for her.
KING   What say'st thou? Ha?
      To pray for her? What, is she crying out?
LOVELL
68   So said her woman, and that her suff'rance made
      Almost each pang a death.

---

46 *moved* aroused   **47** *broken with* conveyed their views to   **49** *fell* deadly
50 *hath* that he has   **52** *convented* summoned   **55** *rest* remain   **62** *deliver*
convey   **68** *suff'rance* suffering

KING   Alas good lady.
SUFFOLK
  God safely quit her of her burden, and   70
  With gentle travail, to the gladding of   71
  Your highness with an heir.
KING   'Tis midnight, Charles.
  Prithee to bed, and in thy prayers remember
  Th' estate of my poor queen. Leave me alone,   74
  For I must think of that which company
  Would not be friendly to.
SUFFOLK   I wish your highness
  A quiet night, and my good mistress will
  Remember in my prayers.
KING   Charles, good night.
                                                    Exit Suffolk.

    Enter Sir Anthony Denny.
  Well, sir, what follows?
DENNY
  Sir, I have brought my lord the archbishop   80
  As you commanded me.
KING   Ha? Canterbury?
DENNY
  Ay, my good lord.
KING   'Tis true: where is he, Denny?
DENNY
  He attends your highness' pleasure.
KING   Bring him to us.
                                                    Exit Denny.
LOVELL   *[Aside]*
  This is about that which the bishop spake.
  I am happily come hither.   85
      Enter Cranmer and Denny.
KING
  Avoid the gallery.   86

---

70 *quit* release   71 *gladding* making happy   74 *estate* condition   85 *happily*
fortunately   86 *Avoid* leave

[Lovell seems to stay.]
                              Ha! I have said. Be gone.
   What!   *Exeunt Lovell and Denny.*
CRANMER   *[Aside]*
       I am fearful. Wherefore frowns he thus?
88   'Tis his aspect of terror. All's not well.
KING
       How now, my lord? You do desire to know
90   Wherefore I sent for you?
CRANMER   *[Kneels.]*   It is my duty
       T' attend your highness' pleasure.
KING   Pray you arise,
       My good and gracious Lord of Canterbury.
       Come, you and I must walk a turn together;
       I have news to tell you. Come, come give me your
          hand.
       Ah, my good lord, I grieve at what I speak
       And am right sorry to repeat what follows.
       I have, and most unwillingly, of late
       Heard many grievous – I do say, my lord,
       Grievous – complaints of you, which being considered,
100   Have moved us and our council, that you shall
       This morning come before us, where I know
102   You cannot with such freedom purge yourself
       But that, till further trial in those charges
       Which will require your answer, you must take
       Your patience to you, and be well contented
106   To make your house our Tower. You, a brother of us,
107   It fits we thus proceed, or else no witness
       Would come against you.
CRANMER   *[Kneels.]*   I humbly thank your highness,
       And am right glad to catch this good occasion

---

88 *aspect of terror* frightening expression   100 *moved* prompted   102 *free-dom* i.e., comprehensive openness; *purge yourself* clear yourself of charges
106 *brother of us* i.e., fellow councillor   107 *fits* is fitting

Most throughly to be winnowed, where my chaff   110
And corn shall fly asunder. For I know
There's none stands under more calumnious tongues   112
Than I myself, poor man.
KING   Stand up, good Canterbury,
Thy truth and thy integrity is rooted
In us, thy friend. Give me thy hand, stand up;
  [Cranmer rises.]
Prithee let's walk. Now by my holidame,   116
What manner of man are you? My lord, I looked   117
You would have given me your petition, that
I should have ta'en some pains to bring together
Yourself and your accusers, and to have heard you   120
Without indurance further.   121
CRANMER   Most dread liege,
The good I stand on is my truth and honesty.
If they shall fail, I with mine enemies   123
Will triumph o'er my person, which I weigh not,   124
Being of those virtues vacant. I fear nothing   125
What can be said against me.
KING   Know you not
How your state stands i' th' world, with the whole
  world?
Your enemies are many and not small; their practices   128
Must bear the same proportion, and not ever   129
The justice and the truth o' th' question carries   130
The due o' th' verdict with it. At what ease
Might corrupt minds procure knaves as corrupt
To swear against you! Such things have been done.
You are potently opposed, and with a malice

---

110 *throughly* thoroughly   112 *stands under* is subject to   116 *by my holidame* i.e., by our Lady   117 *looked* expected   121 *indurance further* further
hardship   123 *shall fail* prove lacking   124 *my person* i.e., my mere self;
weigh not don't value   125 *vacant* lacking   128 *practices* intrigues, plots
129 *bear . . . proportion* be of corresponding magnitude   130 *question*
cause   130–31 *carries . . . it* ensures the just verdict

135 Of as great size. Ween you of better luck,
136 I mean in perjured witness, than your Master,
    Whose minister you are, whiles here he lived
138 Upon this naughty earth? Go to, go to,
    You take a precipice for no leap of danger,
140 And woo your own destruction.
    CRANMER   God and your majesty
    Protect mine innocence, or I fall into
    The trap is laid for me!
    KING   Be of good cheer,
143 They shall no more prevail than we give way to.
    Keep comfort to you, and this morning see
145 You do appear before them. If they shall chance
146 In charging you with matters to commit you,
    The best persuasions to the contrary
    Fail not to use, and with what vehemency
    Th' occasion shall instruct you. If entreaties
150 Will render you no remedy, this ring
    Deliver them, and your appeal to us
    There make before them. Look, the good man weeps:
    He's honest on mine honor! God's blessed mother,
    I swear he is truehearted, and a soul
    None better in my kingdom. Get you gone
    And do as I have bid you.   *[Exit Cranmer.]*
                      He has strangled
    His language in his tears.
        Enter Old Lady.
    GENTLEMAN *[Within]*   Come back: what mean you?
    OLD LADY
    I'll not come back. The tidings that I bring
    Will make my boldness manners. Now good angels
160 Fly o'er thy royal head and shade thy person
    Under their blessed wings!

---

135 *Ween you of* do you imagine 136 *witness* evidence 138 *naughty*
wicked 143 *give way to* allow them scope 145–46 *chance . . . charging you*
venture to charge you 146 *commit* i.e., to the prison of the Tower

KING   Now by thy looks
  I guess thy message. Is the queen delivered?
  Say ay, and of a boy.
OLD LADY   Ay, ay, my liege,
  And of a lovely boy. The God of heaven
  Both now and ever bless her: 'tis a girl
  Promises boys hereafter. Sir, your queen
  Desires your visitation, and to be   167
  Acquainted with this stranger. 'Tis as like you
  As cherry is to cherry.
KING   Lovell!
    [Enter Lovell.]
LOVELL   Sir?
KING
  Give her an hundred marks. I'll to the queen.   170
                                        Exit King.
OLD LADY
  An hundred marks? By this light, I'll ha' more!
  An ordinary groom is for such payment.
  I will have more or scold it out of him.
  Said I for this the girl was like to him?
  I'll have more or else unsay't; and now, while 'tis hot,
  I'll put it to the issue.   *Exit Lady [with Lovell].*   176
                        *

∾ **V.2** *Enter Cranmer, Archbishop of Canterbury*
  [; Pursuivants, Pages, and Footboys at the door].

CRANMER
  I hope I am not too late, and yet the gentleman
  That was sent to me from the council prayed me
  To make great haste. All fast? What means this? Ho!   3

---

167 *visitation* visit   **170** *an hundred marks* (£66, a substantial sum, despite
the old lady's disgruntled response)   **176** *put . . . issue* bring it to a head
  V.2 Outside the council chamber **s.d.** *Pursuivants* junior officers of the
state   **3** *fast* shut (i.e., the doors)

Who waits there? Sure you know me?
   Enter Keeper.
KEEPER   Yes, my lord.
   But yet I cannot help you.
CRANMER
   Why?
KEEPER
   Your grace must wait till you be called for.
   Enter Doctor Butts.
CRANMER   So.
BUTTS   *[Aside]*
   This is a piece of malice. I am glad

9   I came this way so happily. The king
10 Shall understand it presently.   *Exit.*
CRANMER   'Tis Butts,
   The king's physician. As he passed along,
   How earnestly he cast his eyes upon me.
13 Pray heaven he sound not my disgrace, for certain
14 This is of purpose laid by some that hate me
   (God turn their hearts, I never sought their malice)
   To quench mine honor. They would shame to make me
   Wait else at door, a fellow councillor,
   'Mong boys, grooms, and lackeys. But their pleasures
19 Must be fulfilled, and I attend with patience.
   Enter the King and Butts at a window above.
BUTTS
20 I'll show your grace the strangest sight –
KING   What's that, Butts?
BUTTS
   I think your highness saw this many a day.
KING
22 Body a me; where is it?
BUTTS   There, my lord:

---

9 *happily* fortunately   10 *presently* at once   13 *sound* make known   14 *laid* prepared as a trap   19 s.d. (note use of upper stage, not called for elsewhere in the play)   22 *Body a me* (exclamation, "by my body")

The high promotion of his grace of Canterbury,
Who holds his state at door 'mongst pursuivants,   24
Pages, and footboys.
KING   Ha? 'Tis he indeed.
Is this the honor they do one another?
'Tis well there's one above 'em yet. I had thought   27
They had parted so much honesty among 'em –   28
At least good manners – as not thus to suffer
A man of his place and so near our favor   30
To dance attendance on their lordships' pleasures,
And at the door too, like a post with packets.   32
By holy Mary, Butts, there's knavery!
Let 'em alone, and draw the curtain close.   34
We shall hear more anon.   35
      A council table brought in with chairs and stools, and
      placed under the state. Enter Lord Chancellor, places
      himself at the upper end of the table on the left hand, a
      seat being left void above him, as for Canterbury's seat.
      Duke of Suffolk, Duke of Norfolk, Surrey, Lord
      Chamberlain, Gardiner seat themselves in order on
      each side. Cromwell at lower end, as secretary.
CHANCELLOR
Speak to the business, master secretary.
Why are we met in council?
CROMWELL   Please your honors,
The chief cause concerns his grace of Canterbury.
GARDINER
Has he had knowledge of it?   39
CROMWELL   Yes.
NORFOLK   Who waits there?
KEEPER
Without, my noble lords?   40

---

24 *holds his state* maintains his dignity   27 *one above* (1) Henry (?), (2) God
(?)   28 *parted* shared; *honesty* decency   30 *place* rank   32 *post* courier; *packets* mail   34 *Let 'em alone* don't disturb them   35 **s.d.** *state* chair of state   39
had knowledge been informed   40 *Without* outside

GARDINER   Yes.
KEEPER   My lord archbishop,
  And has done half an hour to know your pleasures.
CHANCELLOR
  Let him come in.
KEEPER   Your grace may enter now.
    Cranmer approaches the council table.
CHANCELLOR
  My good lord archbishop, I'm very sorry
44 To sit here at this present and behold
    That chair stand empty; but we are all men
46 In our own natures frail, and capable
    Of our flesh; few are angels; out of which frailty
    And want of wisdom, you, that best should teach us,
49 Have misdemeaned yourself, and not a little:
50 Toward the king first, then his laws, in filling
    The whole realm by your teaching and your chaplains'
    (For so we are informed) with new opinions,
53 Divers and dangerous, which are heresies,
54 And not reformed may prove pernicious.
GARDINER
  Which reformation must be sudden too,
  My noble lords; for those that tame wild horses
  Pace 'em not in their hands to make 'em gentle,
58 But stop their mouths with stubborn bits and spur 'em
59 Till they obey the manage. If we suffer,
60 Out of our easiness and childish pity
  To one man's honor, this contagious sickness,
  Farewell all physic! And what follows then?
63 Commotions, uproars, with a general taint
  Of the whole state, as of late days our neighbors,
65 The upper Germany, can dearly witness,

---

44 *at this present* right now   46–47 *capable . . . flesh* prone to the weaknesses
of the flesh   49 *misdemeaned yourself* conducted yourself improperly   53
Divers various, heterodox   54 *pernicious* extremely harmful   58 *stubborn*
hard   59 *manage* handling (here, rider's control)   60 *easiness* indulgence,
laxity   63 *taint* corruption   65 *upper* i.e., interior

Yet freshly pitied in our memories.
CRANMER
My good lords, hitherto, in all the progress
Both of my life and office, I have labored,
And with no little study, that my teaching   69
And the strong course of my authority   70
Might go one way, and safely, and the end
Was ever to do well; nor is there living
(I speak it with a single heart, my lords)   73
A man that more detests, more stirs against,   74
Both in his private conscience and his place,   75
Defacers of a public peace than I do.   76
Pray heaven the king may never find a heart
With less allegiance in it! Men that make
Envy and crookèd malice nourishment
Dare bite the best. I do beseech your lordships   80
That in this case of justice, my accusers,
Be what they will, may stand forth face to face   82
And freely urge against me.   83
SUFFOLK   Nay, my lord,
That cannot be. You are a councillor,
And by that virtue no man dare accuse you.   85
GARDINER
My lord, because we have business of more moment, 86
We will be short with you. 'Tis his highness' pleasure
And our consent, for better trial of you,
From hence you be committed to the Tower,
Where, being but a private man again,   90
You shall know many dare accuse you boldly,
More than, I fear, you are provided for.
CRANMER
Ah, my good Lord of Winchester, I thank you;

---

69 *study* effort, pains   73 *single* undivided   74 *stirs* takes action   75 *place* office   76 *Defacers* destroyers   82 *Be what they will* whoever they may be   83 *urge* press their charges   85 *by that virtue* by virtue of that   86 *moment* importance

You are always my good friend. If your will pass,
I shall both find your lordship judge and juror,
You are so merciful. I see your end:
'Tis my undoing. Love and meekness, lord,
Become a churchman better than ambition;
99   Win straying souls with modesty again,
100   Cast none away. That I shall clear myself,
101   Lay all the weight ye can upon my patience,
102   I make as little doubt as you do conscience
In doing daily wrongs. I could say more,
But reverence to your calling makes me modest.

GARDINER
105   My lord, my lord, you are a sectary,
106   That's the plain truth. Your painted gloss discovers,
107   To men that understand you, words and weakness.

CROMWELL
My lord of Winchester, you're a little,
By your good favor, too sharp. Men so noble,
110   However faulty, yet should find respect
For what they have been. 'Tis a cruelty
To load a falling man.

GARDINER   Good master secretary,
113   I cry your honor mercy. You may worst
Of all this table say so.

CROMWELL   Why, my lord?

GARDINER
Do not I know you for a favorer
116   Of this new sect? Ye are not sound.

CROMWELL   Not sound?

GARDINER
Not sound, I say.

CROMWELL   Would you were half so honest!

---

99 *modesty* moderation   101 *Lay . . . can* exert all the pressure you can   102
I make . . . conscience I have as little doubt as you have scruple   105 *sectary*
adherent of a heretical sect   106 *painted gloss* specious rhetoric; *discovers* re-
veals   107 *words* mere words   110 *find* meet with   113 *I cry . . . mercy* I
beg your honor's pardon; *worst* with least cause   116 *sound* loyal

Men's prayers then would seek you, not their fears.
GARDINER
  I shall remember this bold language.
CROMWELL   Do.
  Remember your bold life too.   *120*
CHANCELLOR   That is too much.
  Forbear for shame, my lords.
GARDINER   I have done.
CROMWELL   And I.
CHANCELLOR
  Then thus for you, my lord: it stands agreed,
  I take it, by all voices, that forthwith   *123*
  You be conveyed to th' Tower a prisoner,   *124*
  There to remain till the king's further pleasure
  Be known unto us. Are you all agreed, lords?
ALL
  We are.
CRANMER   Is there no other way of mercy
  But I must needs to th' Tower, my lords?
GARDINER   What other
  Would you expect? You are strangely troublesome.   *129*
  Let some o' th' guard be ready there!   *130*
    Enter the Guard.
CRANMER   For me?
  Must I go like a traitor thither?   *131*
GARDINER   Receive him
  And see him safe i' th' Tower.
CRANMER   Stay, good my lords,
  I have a little yet to say. Look there, my lords.
  By virtue of that ring I take my cause
  Out of the gripes of cruel men and give it   *135*
  To a most noble judge, the king my master.
CHAMBERLAIN
  This is the king's ring.

---

123 *voices* votes   124 *conveyed* escorted   129 *strangely* extraordinarily   131 *Receive* take   135 *gripes* clutches

SURREY   'Tis no counterfeit.

SUFFOLK
'Tis the right ring, by heav'n! I told ye all,
When we first put this dangerous stone a-rolling,
140 'Twould fall upon ourselves.

NORFOLK   Do you think, my lords,
The king will suffer but the little finger
Of this man to be vexed?

CHAMBERLAIN   'Tis now too certain,
143 How much more is his life in value with him.
144 Would I were fairly out on't!

CROMWELL   My mind gave me,
145 In seeking tales and informations
Against this man, whose honesty the devil
And his disciples only envy at,
148 Ye blew the fire that burns ye: now have at ye!
    Enter King, frowning on them; takes his seat.

GARDINER
Dread sovereign, how much are we bound to heaven
150 In daily thanks, that gave us such a prince,
Not only good and wise but most religious;
One that in all obedience makes the church
The chief aim of his honor, and to strengthen
154 That holy duty out of dear respect,
His royal self in judgment comes to hear
The cause betwixt her and this great offender.

KING
157 You were ever good at sudden commendations,
Bishop of Winchester. But know I come not
To hear such flattery now, and in my presence
160 They are too thin and base to hide offenses;
To me you cannot reach. You play the spaniel,
And think with wagging of your tongue to win me.

---

143 *in value* esteemed   144 *My . . . me* I had a misgiving   145 *tales and informations* incriminating hearsay   148 *have at ye* look out for yourselves
154 *dear* heartfelt   157 *sudden commendations* impromptu compliments

But whatsoe'er thou tak'st me for, I'm sure
Thou hast a cruel nature and a bloody.
     [To Cranmer]
Good man, sit down. Now let me see the proudest
He, that dares most, but wag his finger at thee.   166
By all that's holy, he had better starve   167
Than but once think his place becomes thee not.
SURREY
     May it please your grace –
KING   No, sir, it does not please me.
     I had thought I had had men of some understanding   *170*
     And wisdom of my council; but I find none.
     Was it discretion, lords, to let this man,
     This good man (few of you deserve that title),
     This honest man, wait like a lousy footboy   174
     At chamber door? And one as great as you are?
     Why, what a shame was this? Did my commission   176
     Bid ye so far forget yourselves? I gave ye
     Power as he was a councillor to try him,
     Not as a groom. There's some of ye, I see,
     More out of malice than integrity,   *180*
     Would try him to the utmost, had ye mean,   181
     Which ye shall never have while I live.
CHANCELLOR   Thus far,
     My most dread sovereign, may it like your grace   183
     To let my tongue excuse all. What was purposed
     Concerning his imprisonment was rather
     (If there be faith in men) meant for his trial
     And fair purgation to the world than malice,   187
     I'm sure, in me.
KING   Well, well, my lords, respect him.
     Take him, and use him well; he's worthy of it.
     I will say thus much for him: if a prince   *190*

---

166 *He* man   167 *starve* die   174 *lousy* covered with lice   176 *shame* inflic-
tion of dishonor   181 *try* harass, afflict   183 *like* please   187 *purgation*
clearing of himself

191 May be beholding to a subject, I
 Am for his love and service so to him.
 Make me no more ado, but all embrace him.
 Be friends for shame, my lords. My Lord of Canter-
  bury,
 I have a suit which you must not deny me;
 That is, a fair young maid that yet wants baptism,
. You must be godfather and answer for her.
CRANMER
 The greatest monarch now alive may glory
 In such an honor. How may I deserve it
200 That am a poor and humble subject to you?
201 KING Come, come, my lord, you'd spare your spoons!
202 You shall have two noble partners with you, the old
 Duchess of Norfolk and Lady Marquis Dorset. Will
 these please you?
 Once more, my Lord of Winchester, I charge you
 Embrace and love this man.
GARDINER   With a true heart
207 And brother love I do it.
CRANMER   And let heaven
 Witness how dear I hold this confirmation.
KING
 Good man, those joyful tears show thy true heart.
210 The common voice I see is verified
 Of thee, which says thus: "Do my Lord of Canterbury
212 A shrewd turn, and he's your friend for ever."
 Come, lords, we trifle time away. I long
 To have this young one made a Christian.
 As I have made ye one, lords, one remain;
 So I grow stronger, you more honor gain. *Exeunt.*

           *

---

191 *beholding* indebted **201** *you'd . . . spoons* i.e., you'd economize by not giving the traditional apostle spoons to godchildren (Henry is teasing Cranmer) **202** *partners* i.e., fellow godparents **207** *brother love* brotherly love **212** *shrewd* bad

❧ **V.3** *Noise and tumult within. Enter Porter and his*
Man.

PORTER   You'll leave your noise anon, ye rascals! Do you
   take the court for Parish Garden? Ye rude slaves, leave   2
   your gaping!   3
[ONE]   *Within*   Good master porter, I belong to th' larder.   4
PORTER   Belong to th' gallows and be hanged, ye rogue!
   Is this a place to roar in? Fetch me a dozen crab-tree
   staves, and strong ones; these are but switches to 'em: 7
   I'll scratch your heads. You must be seeing christenings?
   Do you look for ale and cakes here, you rude rascals?   9
MAN
   Pray, sir, be patient; 'tis as much impossible,   10
   Unless we sweep 'em from the door with cannons,
   To scatter 'em as 'tis to make 'em sleep
   On May Day morning, which will never be.   13
   We may as well push against Paul's as stir 'em.   14
PORTER   How got they in, and be hanged?
MAN
   Alas I know not, how gets the tide in!
   As much as one sound cudgel of four foot
   (You see the poor remainder) could distribute,
   I made no spare, sir.   19
PORTER   You did nothing, sir.
MAN
   I am not Samson, nor Sir Guy, nor Colebrand,   20
   To mow 'em down before me. But if I spared any
   That had a head to hit, either young or old,
   He or she, cuckold or cuckold maker,

V.3 The palace courtyard   2 *Parish Garden* Paris Garden (a London venue
for cruel, unruly sports like bearbaiting and bullbaiting)   3 *gaping* bawling
4 *belong to* i.e., am employed in   7 *switches* thin canes   9 *ale and cakes* (traditional festive fare)   13 *May Day* May 1 (traditionally, a day of festivity)
14 *Paul's* Saint Paul's Cathedral   19 *made no spare* didn't stint   20
Samson . . . Colebrand (Samson, Guy of Warwick, and Colebrand – a giant
slain by Guy in a popular story – were all noted for great strength)

24 Let me ne'er hope to see a chine again,
25 And that I would not for a cow, God save her.
    [ONE] *Within* Do you hear, master porter?
    PORTER I shall be with you presently, good master
    puppy. Keep the door close, sirrah.
    MAN What would you have me do?
30 PORTER What should you do but knock 'em down by
31 th' dozens? Is this Moorfields to muster in? Or have we
32 some strange Indian with the great tool come to court,
33 the women so besiege us? Bless me, what a fry of forni-
    cation is at door! On my Christian conscience this one
    christening will beget a thousand; here will be father,
    godfather, and all together.
37 MAN The spoons will be the bigger, sir. There is a fellow
38 somewhat near the door, he should be a brazier by his
39 face, for o' my conscience twenty of the dog days now
40 reign in's nose. All that stand about him are under the
41 line; they need no other penance. That firedrake did I
    hit three times on the head, and three times was his
43 nose discharged against me; he stands there like a mor-
44 tar piece to blow us. There was a haberdasher's wife of
45 small wit near him, that railed upon me till her pinked
    porringer fell off her head, for kindling such a combus-
    tion in the state. I missed the meteor once and hit that
48 woman, who cried out "Clubs," when I might see from

---

24 *chine* joint of beef 25 *not for a cow* (common expression, meaning "not
for anything") 31 *Moorfields* (a park where military training was conducted); *muster* assemble (as for military training) 32 *strange Indian . . .
tool* (North American Indian, already apparently the subject of European leg-
ends or fantasies regarding extraordinary penis size) 33–34 *fry of fornication* swarm of would-be fornicators 37 *spoons* i.e., christening spoons (cf.
V.2.201) 38 *brazier* brass maker 39 *dog days* i.e., hottest season (July 13–
August 15), when the Dog Star, Sirius, rises at the same time as the sun 40
reign in's nose i.e., his nose has a fiery red glow ·41 *line* equator; *firedrake* meteor (still referring to the red nose) 43 *discharged* fired (like a cannon)
43–44 *like a mortar piece* i.e., gaping upward 44 *blow us* blow us up; *haberdasher* purveyor of small garments, ribbons, etc. 45–46 *pinked porringer*
round cap ornamented with perforations, looking like a porridge dish 48
Clubs (the call that summoned apprentices to start or stop a fight)

far some forty truncheoners draw to her succor, which   49
were the hope o' th' Strond, where she was quartered.   50
They fell on, I made good my place. At length they   51
came to th' broomstaff to me; I defied 'em still, when   52
suddenly a file of boys behind 'em, loose shot, delivered   53
such a shower of pebbles that I was fain to draw mine   54
honor in and let 'em win the work. The devil was   55
amongst 'em I think surely.

PORTER   These are the youths that thunder at a playhouse and fight for bitten apples, that no audience but
the tribulation of Tower Hill or the limbs of Lime-   59
house, their dear brothers, are able to endure. I have   60
some of 'em in Limbo Patrum, and there they are like   61
to dance these three days, besides the running banquet   62
of two beadles that is to come.

    Enter Lord Chamberlain.

CHAMBERLAIN
Mercy o' me, what a multitude are here!
They grow still too; from all parts they are coming
As if we kept a fair here. Where are these porters,
These lazy knaves? Y' have made a fine hand, fellows!   67
There's a trim rabble let in; are all these   68
Your faithful friends o' th' suburbs? We shall have   69
Great store of room, no doubt, left for the ladies   70
When they pass back from the christening.   71

PORTER   An't   please
    your honor,

---

49 *truncheoners* cudgel bearers **50** *Strond* Strand (a fashionable street in London) **51** *fell on* attacked; *made good my place* held my ground **52** *broomstaff* i.e., close quarters **53** *loose shot* marksmen not attached to a company **54** *fain* obliged **55** *work* fortification **59** *tribulation of Tower Hill* (a particular gang of ruffians) (?); *limbs* youths (*of Limehouse* possibly referring to another youth gang) **61** *Limbo Patrum* prison (refers to a region near hell in traditional Catholic belief) **62–63** *running . . . beadles* i.e., whipping by public officials known as beadles, the offender being forced to run through the streets while being whipped **67** *made a fine hand* done a nice job (ironic) **68** *trim* elegant (ironic) **69** *suburbs* areas outside city jurisdiction **71** *An't* if it

We are but men, and what so many may do,
Not being torn apieces, we have done.

74 An army cannot rule 'em.

CHAMBERLAIN   As I live,
75 If the king blame me for't, I'll lay ye all
76 By th' heels, and suddenly; and on your heads
77 Clap round fines for neglect. You're lazy knaves,
78 And here ye lie baiting of bombards when
Ye should do service. Hark, the trumpets sound!
80 Th' are come already from the christening.
81 Go break among the press, and find a way out
82 To let the troop pass fairly, or I'll find
83 A Marshalsea shall hold ye play these two months.

PORTER
Make way there for the princess!

MAN   You great fellow,
85 Stand close up, or I'll make your head ache!

PORTER
86 You i' th' chamblet, get up o' th' rail,
87 I'll peck you o'er the pales else!   *Exeunt.*

*

~ **V.4** *Enter Trumpets, sounding; then two Aldermen,*
Lord Mayor, Garter, Cranmer, Duke of Norfolk with
his marshal's staff, Duke of Suffolk, two Noblemen
bearing great standing bowls for the christening gifts;
then four Noblemen bearing a canopy, under which
the Duchess of Norfolk, godmother, bearing the child
richly habited in a mantle, etc., train borne by a Lady;

---

74 *rule* control   75–76 *lay . . . heels* clap you in the stocks   76 *suddenly* immediately   77 *Clap* impose; *round* heavy   78 *baiting of bombards* drinking deep (out of leathern bottles)   81 *among the press* through the crowd   82 *fairly* in orderly fashion   83 *Marshalsea* prison in Southwark   85 *close up* out of the way   86 *chamblet* camlet (a rich fabric made of goat's hair)   87 *peck you . . . pales* pitch you over the rails (barricades)
    V.4 The palace **s.d.** *Trumpets* trumpeters; *Garter* (see note on IV.1.36, item 5); *standing bowls* bowls with legs; *habited* garbed

then follows the Marchioness Dorset, the other god-
mother, and Ladies. The troop pass once about the
stage, and Garter speaks.

GARTER   Heaven, from thy endless goodness, send pros-   1
perous life, long and ever happy, to the high and
mighty princess of England, Elizabeth.
Flourish. Enter King and Guard.
CRANMER   *[Kneels.]*
And to your royal grace and the good queen,
My noble partners and myself thus pray   5
All comfort, joy in this most gracious lady,
Heaven ever laid up to make parents happy,
May hourly fall upon ye!
KING   · Thank you, good lord arch-
bishop.
What is her name?
CRANMER   Elizabeth.
KING   Stand up, lord.
[Cranmer rises. The King kisses the child.]
With this kiss take my blessing. God protect thee,   10
Into whose hand I give thy life.
CRANMER   Amen.
KING
My noble gossips, y' have been too prodigal;   12
I thank ye heartily. So shall this lady,
When she has so much English.
CRANMER   Let me speak, sir,
For heaven now bids me, and the words I utter
Let none think flattery, for they'll find 'em truth.
This royal infant – heaven still move about her! –   17
Though in her cradle, yet now promises
Upon this land a thousand thousand blessings,

1–3 *Heaven . . . Elizabeth* (a formula used on such occasions) 5 *partners* fellow godparents 12 *gossips* godparents; *prodigal* generous 17 *heaven . . .
her* may God be always near her

20   Which time shall bring to ripeness. She shall be
        (But few now living can behold that goodness)
        A pattern to all princes living with her
23   And all that shall succeed. Saba was never
        More covetous of wisdom and fair virtue
        Than this pure soul shall be. All princely graces
26   That mold up such a mighty piece as this is,
        With all the virtues that attend the good,
        Shall still be doubled on her. Truth shall nurse her,
29   Holy and heavenly thoughts still counsel her;
30   She shall be loved and feared; her own shall bless her;
        Her foes shake like a field of beaten corn
        And hang their heads with sorrow. Good grows with
          her;
        In her days every man shall eat in safety
        Under his own vine what he plants, and sing
        The merry songs of peace to all his neighbors.
        God shall be truly known, and those about her
37   From her shall read the perfect ways of honor,
        And by those claim their greatness, not by blood.
        Nor shall this peace sleep with her, but as when
40   The bird of wonder dies, the maiden phoenix,
41   Her ashes new create another heir
42   As great in admiration as herself,
        So shall she leave her blessedness to one
44   (When heaven shall call her from this cloud of dark-
          ness)
        Who from the sacred ashes of her honor
        Shall starlike rise, as great in fame as she was,

---

23 *Saba* biblical Queen of Sheba, who visited Solomon on account of his reputed wisdom   26 *mold . . . piece* constitute so great a work (person)   29
still always   30 *own* own people   37 *read* learn   40 *maiden phoenix* (Elizabeth had often been compared to the mythical, self-regenerating phoenix)
41 *heir* (James I, the reigning monarch at the time *Henry VIII* was written,
inheriting from Elizabeth, but not as the natural offspring of the queen, who
died unmarried)   42 *As great in admiration* i.e., just as wondrous   44 *cloud
of darkness* i.e., this dark, mortal condition

And so stand fixed. Peace, plenty, love, truth, terror,
That were the servants to this chosen infant,
Shall then be his, and like a vine grow to him.
Wherever the bright sun of heaven shall shine,   50
His honor and the greatness of his name
Shall be, and make new nations. He shall flourish
And like a mountain cedar reach his branches
To all the plains about him. Our children's children
Shall see this, and bless heaven.
KING   Thou speakest wonders.
CRANMER
She shall be, to the happiness of England,
An aged princess; many days shall see her,
And yet no day without a deed to crown it.
Would I had known no more! But she must die –
She must, the saints must have her – yet a virgin.   60
A most unspotted lily shall she pass
To th' ground, and all the world shall mourn her.
KING
O lord archbishop,
Thou hast made me now a man. Never before   64
This happy child did I get anything.   65
This oracle of comfort has so pleased me
That when I am in heaven I shall desire
To see what this child does, and praise my Maker.
I thank ye all. To you, my good lord mayor,
And you good brethren, I am much beholding.   70
I have received much honor by your presence,
And ye shall find me thankful. Lead the way, lords,
Ye must all see the queen, and she must thank ye;
She will be sick else. This day, no man think   74
'Has business at his house, for all shall stay: 75
This little one shall make it Holy Day.   *Exeunt.*
                         ✳

---

64 *a man* i.e., a happy, thriving man   65 *get* beget   70 *beholding* indebted
74 *sick* unhappy   75 *'Has* i.e., he has

THE EPILOGUE

∾ **Epi.**

'Tis ten to one this play can never please
All that are here. Some come to take their ease
And sleep an act or two, but those we fear
W' have frighted with our trumpets, so 'tis clear
5   They'll say 'tis naught; others to hear the city
Abused extremely, and to cry "That's witty,"
7   Which we have not done neither; that I fear
All the expected good w' are like to hear .
For this play at this time, is only in
10   The merciful construction of good women,
For such a one we showed 'em. If they smile
And say 'twill do, I know within a while
13   All the best men are ours; for 'tis ill hap,
14   If they hold when their ladies bid 'em clap.

Epilogue   5 *naught* bad   7 *that* so that   10 *construction* interpretation   13 *ill hap* an unhappy circumstance   14 *hold* hold back